JACKIE: BEYOND THE MYTH OF CAMELOT

JACKIE: BEYOND THE MYTH OF CAMELOT

A Passion for Artists & Authors

K.L. Kelleher

To order additional copies of this book, contact:
Xlibris Corporation
1-888-7-XLIBRIS
www.Xlibris.com
Orders@Xlibris.com

CONTENTS

Illustrations and Photographs 13

A Remembrance of Camelot 17

Jackie On The Eve of the Election 31

Cultural Exchange: A Kennedy Mission 47

Apotheosis In Paris and Vienna 56

A Shared Love for Artists & Writers 72

A Journey to Cambodia 99

Becoming A Book Editor 115

Photography Adventures 135

Hammersmith Farm and Tsar Nicholas 147

Saving the Temples: Dendur and Grand Central 158

Impressions of India 169

Peter Sis After The Velvet Revolution 184

An American Author: Louis Auchincloss 192

The Renaissance Lady From Avignon 199

In memory of my Italian mother Genevieve Listro Kelleher's sheer joy when she went to see Leonardo da Vinci's *Mona Lisa* at the National Gallery of Art in 1963. Her passionate tales about *"The Great Lady"* have captivated me all my life.

RALPH WALDO EMERSON

CHARACTER

The sun set, but set not her hope:
Stars rose; her faith was earlier up:
Fixed on the enormous galaxy,
Deeper and older seemed her eye;
And matched her sufferance sublime
The taciturnity of time.
She spoke, with words more soft than rain
That Brought the Age of Gold again:
Her actions won such reverence sweet
As hid all measure of the feat.

Special Thanks To:

*Greg Brousseau, Eric Payson and my agent Fifi Oscard
for being loyal and patient friends to me.*

ILLUSTRATIONS AND PHOTOGRAPHS

Bookcover:

The Bouvier gardens at *Lasata* and Senator Kennedy and Jacqueline Bouvier sailing in Hyannis Port the summer before their wedding in Newport.

Frontispiece:

Sketch of Michelangelo's *The Prophecy of Isaiah*, Sistine Chapel, 1534

Page 21:

Alex Gottfried's cover design for Naguib Mahfouz's American edition of *Palace of Desire*, Jacqueline Onassis commissioning editor.

Page 40:

Jacqueline and Lee Bouvier in East Hampton.

Page 50:

Cover of the volume of speeches *The Strategy of Peace* written by Senator John F. Kennedy.

Page 67:

Andre Malraux selecting photographs, above Jacqueline Kennedy with Charles DeGaulle at the Versailles state dinner in the Hall of Mirrors

Page 73:

Winston Churchill cartoon "I'm not afraid of Hitler!"

Page 79:

Cover of the historical biography book *Profiles In Courage* written by Senator John F. Kennedy and the 1960 Democratic National Convention

Page 84:

Washington Post's cartoon of Aristotle Onassis and the international jet-set on his yacht the *Christina*

Page 86:

President Kennedy and Jacqueline at the Nobel Peace Prize dinner with honored guests poet Robert Frost and Mary Hemingway above the ancient Greek theater *Herodus Atticus* in Athens.

Page 98:

Robert F. Kennedy and First Lady Jacqueline walk in President Kennedy's funeral, Senator Kennedy in Los Angeles, Ethel Kennedy's expression of grief after the shooting of her husband, Senator Robert Kennedy and Ethel Kennedy visiting Coretta Scott King, and Prince Sihanouk meeting Jacqueline Kennedy in Cambodia in 1967.

Page 114:

Marc Riboud's photographs of Vietnam, Angkor Wat in Cambodia and the mountain region in China *Capital of Heaven.*

Page 123:

Frontispiece photograph taken by Vladimir Bliokh of Judith Jamison for her autobiography *Dancing Spirit.*

Page 127:

Book cover of Martha Graham's autobiography *Blood Memory.*

Page 132:

Book cover of Jonathan Cott's history *Isis and Osiris.*

Page 136:

Back cover of photography memoir with the photographers Toni Frissell's self-portrait, and Frissell photograph of Senator Kennedy and Jacqueline Bouvier's 1953 wedding.

Page 148:

August 17, 2000 *New York Times* headline, "Nicholas II and Family Canonized for Passion". Photographs of Hugh D. Auchincloss, and George Balanchine and Igor Stravinsky choreographing a ballet together.

Page 155:

Book cover of Edvard Radzinsky's biography of *Stalin.*

Page 161:

Book cover of Christine Desroches Noblecourt's memoir of the international effort to preserve the Nubian temples in Egypt from 1960 to 1967.

Page 171:

Jacqueline Kennedy and the Maharani of Jaipur Ayesha in Jaipur, and a Muhgal miniature painting in Jacqueline Onassis' art collection.

Page 188:

Peter Sis' early drawing to illustrate *The Three Golden Keys,* view of the Charles Bridge in Prague, photographs of Peter Sis and his editor Mrs. Onassis, and the postcards she mailed to Peter Sis of Arcimboldo's painting *The Librarian.*

Page 195:

The Cat and The King's back book cover drawing of Louis Auchincloss, and the gardens at Versailles.

Page 205:

The Popes' summer palace at Avignon and photograph of Carly Simon

A REMEMBRANCE OF CAMELOT

The way Jacqueline Onassis lived is revealing of her mission in life. Her spirited passion transformed writers and artists' dreams into cherished traditions in American life. When President Kennedy was assassinated, with unfaltering grace and dignity, she endured times of sorrow and national tragedy. Later on, Jackie became a book editor to continue her passions and dreams. When she read in French translation *The Cairo Trilogy* by novelist Naguib Mahfouz, she admired his epic tale of Egyptian life during its struggle for independence from British rule. She told editorial director of *Publisher's Weekly*, John F. Baker, she thought to herself, "We've got to have that." One wonders how many times in the past did she consider what other cultural influences *Americans* had to have?

Jackie offers her affinity for the author, "I've always loved the cultures of the Mediterranean, and I lived in Greece . . . I just clicked with some other Mediterranean writers like Nikos Kazantzakis." In 1992, she encouraged the Egyptian novelist, Mahfouz, to write a lyrical short story for a large book of Robert Lyons photography in *Egyptian Time*. Mahfouz writes about the human condition: "A short period, but bearing unnumbered embryonic possibilities. It bears witness to eternal questions to love, sex, friendship, honor, life, death, the glorious Presence of the Almighty, basic themes that develop and diversify life, taking from the rich sea rushing waves and vast horizons. These still scatter to

us longings and meditations, dreams and deeds, self-absorption
and exuberance. Never relinquishing our everlasting wish to discover the lamp that will light the path of fate."

Two years after *The Cairo Trilogy* was published in America,
Jackie died on May 19th, 1994. Around the world, the television
cameras exploded into a nostalgic frenzy of film clips. Jackie's be-
witching glamour poured out of the television, so those far away
could wonder at the mystery of her life. John Kennedy appeared
before her neighbors, and friends: "Last night at around 10:15,
my mother passed on . . . surrounded by her friends and family
and her books . . . and she did it on her own terms, and now she's
in God's hands." He thanked the assembled mourners, then dis-
appeared into 1040 Fifth Avenue.

Caroline and John carefully planned their mother's funeral
according to her wishes. They asked Father Modrys to speak on
the biblical readings from the Jewish philosopher-prophet Isaiah.
Isaiah belonged to the tribe of Judah, one of the ten tribes of the
Kingdom of Israel. He became an advisor to the reforming king
Hezekiah who ruled Judah, a nation-kingdom from 715 to 687.
Isaiah is often called 'the world's first evangelist' and was thought
to be one of the first literate prophets. His prophecy describes a
promised future invoking religious tolerance, peace and justice,
and a time when all 'nations' lived together peacefully in the symbolic holy city of Jerusalem.

On the day of her funeral mass, no television cameras were
permitted inside the Church of St. Ignatius Loyola on Park Avenue
and 84th Street. But for her neighbors, friends, and distant admirers who came to bid Jacqueline farewell, there was a sound
system to transmit the mass outdoors. The voice of the priest read
a passage by the Scottish writer of legend, Sir Walter Raleigh:

Give me my scallop-shell of quiet
My staff of faith to walk upon,
My scrip of joy, immortal diet.
My bottle of salvation,
My gown of glory, hope's true gage;
And thus I'll take my pilgrimage.

Jackie's family members and friends were gathered inside the church: Ethel and Senator Edward M. Kennedy, Maurice Tempelsman, Louis and Yusha Auchincloss, her sister Lee Radziwill, and many friends from the White House years; Rose and Bill Styron, Kitty and John Kenneth Galbraith and the steadfast Ted Sorenson, who carry on their faces the promise of President Kennedy. Everyone there seemed to know some fantastic tale of her life's journey, a cavalcade of storytellers; Karl Katz and Mike Nichols, the writer Jane Hitchcock, her authors; the dancer Judith Jamison, the singer Carly Simon, Bill Moyers, and her friends who inspired America to save Grand Central, Fred Papert, Kent Barwick, Ashton Hawkins and so many others.

Her death inspired many to look back to her White House adventure, Jackie hailed *Camelot*. People often wonder why did she *request* Theodore White in 1963 to employ this metaphor for her shared dreams with President John F. Kennedy? She knew it was a legend of gallantry, filled with honor, illusion and a fantasy utopia. King Arthur's Camelot, a story to inspire young children to dream of conquering evil, has faded as popular mythology. J.K. Rowling's tales of *Harry Potter*, the mythology currently in vogue, captivates young people today, but at one time every boy dreamed of becoming King Arthur. Jackie knew that her husband loved the adventurous tales of brave knights as a boy. The Kennedy's international prominence coincided with the golden age of musical theater; the Marine Band often played songs from *South Pacific*, *My Fair Lady*, *The King and I*, and *The Sound of Music* at the Kennedy White House. Considering Jackie's love of performing arts and music, her metaphor might have been *The Sound of Music*. But *Camelot's*

Broadway premiere, December 1960, celebrated John F. Kennedy's presidential inauguration.

The tale of King Arthur begins on his wedding day, he rises to give this speech "And rose the king and spake to all the Table Round, and charged them to be ever true and noble knights, to do neither outrage nor murder, nor any unjust violence, and always to flee treason; also by no means ever to be cruel, but give mercy unto him that ask for mercy, upon pain of forfeiting the liberty of his court for evermore . . . at all times, on pain of death, to give all succor unto ladies and young damsels; and lastly, never to take part in any wrongful quarrel, for reward or payment. And to all this he swore them knight by knight . . . And so with prayer and blessing, and high words of cheer, he instituted the most noble order of the Round Table, whereto the best and bravest knights in all the world sought afterwards to find admission . . ." Jackie felt that the promise of a better world and King Arthur's prayer gave allure to the Kennedy's political beliefs.

At Jackie's funeral mass, Judith Jamison, the dancer, who created the book *Dancing Spirit* at the urging of her editor Jacqueline Onassis, was seated in the church. Judith reflects on her impressions of the mass, "For me, it seemed absolutely reflective of her, and her tastes. As soon as I heard *Faure Requiem*, that was it. I was no good after that . . . And the priest kept saying *Jacqueline* . . . it sounded wonderful. It was all so wonderful."

John Kennedy gave the *Introduction to the Liturgy of the Word*, "we struggled to find ones that captured my mother's essence." In profound simplicity, he described that "three things came to mind over and over again . . . they were her love of words, the bonds of home and family, and her spirit of adventure." John quoted from the *First Reading: Isaiah*, "On this mountain the Lord of hosts will provide for all peoples . . . he will destroy the veil that veils all peoples . . . he will destroy death forever . . . will wipe away the tears from all faces."

WINNER OF THE NOBEL PRIZE FOR LITERATURE

NAGUIB MAHFOUZ

PALACE *of* DESIRE

"MAHFOUZ TELLS THE STORY OF PALACE OF DESIRE WITH
SENSITIVITY AND HUMOR, OFFERING DEEP INSIGHTS INTO THE HUMAN CONDITION."
— PHILADELPHIA INQUIRER

Diana Vreeland, George Balanchine, Toni Frissell, Rudolph Nureyev and many other old friends died before Jackie. As if an emissary sent by the spirit of her mentor, Deborah Turbeville attended the funeral. Over a decade earlier, Diana Vreeland introduced the fashion photographer, Turbeville, to Jackie and the book *Unseen Versailles* was conceived and published. Deborah recalls her vision of Jackie, "Oh for *Balanchine*, she was his Medici. She was a real friend who tried to help him work out these things that were such a problem. All the ideas he had, and all the things that he wanted to do, even in this country, there wasn't enough money for the New York City Ballet. She had such an intelligence and such an awareness of who people were. She studied to see who the people were who lived at the same moment that she was living, to search out those people who she admired. And when she came across them, she tried to find some way of working with them. Then she became their great patron and their great friend. She was incredibly supportive. If she found these people and they couldn't do all the things she admired them for, then she would find a way to help them."

George Plimpton, aware of the way Jackie would adopt people she admired, remarked some time after the mass, "To my utter surprise, Jane Hitchcock read one of the prayers at the funeral service. I didn't even know that she knew Jackie and I've known Jane for years. What was it? Maybe Jackie enjoyed this very bright, funny woman." Jane Hitchcock read the *Responsorial Psalm: 23rd Psalm, The Lord is my Shepherd, I shall not want.* "He leadeth me in the paths of righteousness . . . though I walk through the valley of the shadow of death, I will fear no evil: for thou art with me . . ."

Mike Nichols read from the book of *Revelation*, "I saw a new heaven and a new earth. The former heaven and the former earth had passed away, and the sea was no more. I also saw the holy city, a new Jerusalem. He will wipe every tear from their eyes, and there shall be no more death or mourning, wailing or pain, for the old order has passed away . . .'Behold, I make all things new. I am the

Alpha and the Omega, the beginning and the end. To the thirsty I will give a gift from the spring of life-giving water . . .'"

Kitty Galbraith once told a story about Jackie and Mike Nichols, who became her friend in the sixties, and was a neighbor on Martha's Vineyard. "A couple of years after the President's death, she wanted to see a play that opened in Boston. Mike Nichols was the director, and we were to have dinner after the theater. But there was bad weather and Jackie was delayed at Laguardia. So, Mike and I got word that she was to meet us at the theater. They held the play for about four or five minutes. But nothing happened."

"Then the lights went out, so they snuck her in. And when the lights came on, somebody had recognized her and we heard these whispers, *Jacqueline Kennedy*. After the performance, she knew the press would be there. So, she said to me, 'Kitty, no matter what, when you see a camera, you get between me and Mike and the camera.'"

"So, when she was leaving, I had to put my face in front of hers getting into the taxi. I felt so embarrassed, but it was so funny, so the press wouldn't get a picture of her and Mike and then make some kind of a story out of it."

Kitty Galbraith summed things up when she said, "Who wouldn't love to be all the things that Jackie was, so cultivated, so talented,—and she was a wonderful editor. She was very amusing and very loyal to her friends." John Kenneth Galbraith added, "There's a larger word there, too. She had a certain inherent charm, which is hard to analyze, but was very much a part of her."

When the radiant and intelligent, Jacqueline Bouvier married Jack Kennedy, a new world seemed to emerge. Comrade Stalin's death on March 5, 1953 signaled an end to fascist dictatorships and the Russian holocaust. Winston Churchill was alive and well, and a post-World War II, prosperous American way of life had arrived. Yusha Auchincloss described Jackie's wedding in Newport as if an Irishman had invaded the changing of the guard in Newport society, "the wedding was a publicity spectacle, promoted as a fairy tale by the groom's father, Joseph P. Kennedy . . ." *Harper's Bazaar* sent Jackie's friend Toni Frissell to photograph the society wedding. When Toni tried to send in her pictures, her editor, Carmel Snow gasped "Don't bother to send them! There's been such notoriety they are worthless to *Harper's Bazaar*!" Yusha Auchincloss regrets, "That huge crowd, and the behind-the-scenes maneuvering of her father was just a total disaster, not what Jackie wanted at all! But between her mother and Joe Kennedy she just lost control of the whole thing." Yet, like the marriage ceremony of King Arthur and Guinevere, the mythology of Camelot seemed to descend upon this romantic couple the very day they married. The Arthurian legend forms a mythology with a love match, " . . . and when they came to Camelot, King Arthur made great joy, and with a great retinue he met Guinevere, led her through the streets, in the midst of the ringing of church bells . . ."

Jackie admired all the father figures in her life. She dearly loved her own father, Jack Bouvier, her grandfathers *Grampy Jack* and James T. Lee, her step-father Hugh D. Auchincloss, and her father-in-law Joseph P. Kennedy. In all these men, Jackie and Lee's first cousin, John Davis, seems to have found a shared belief, that was instilled in her as a child. Jackie's Bouvier grandfather, "was an extraordinary leader of children and we all loved him." John Davis recalls, "He used to read a passage from Thomas Babington Macaulay when telling us about our ancestors. 'A people which takes no pride in the noble achievements of remote ancestors will never achieve anything to be remembered with pride by remote descendants.' And that would be one of the rituals that he would go through. I remember it made a great impression."

The reading from the fourth gospel with its image of the Father's house with many dwelling places inspires a vision of Jackie entering a house with rooms leading to exciting possibilities. As a young girl, she lived in two great forty acre estates, after her mother Janet divorced Jack Bouvier and remarried Hugh D. Auchincloss. In the book, "Pictures of Horse and English Life" by A. J. Munnings published in 1927, Jackie wrote the inscription, "given to me by

Uncle Hugh, March 27, 1963 because I loved growing up at Merrywood." Both Merrywood and Hammersmith Farm were designed to evoke the feeling that the opening of doors into high-ceilinged great rooms with book-lined libraries had the power to make your wildest dreams come true. She once wrote to her step-brother Yusha in 1945, "It was very lonely the last day at Merrywood with you gone and Lee at school. I walked over the whole place and nearly burst loving it—I wrote about it in my diary."

Edwin Schlossberg, Caroline's husband, spoke in his own words, "For the nation and the people whom she served and then sustained—and who gave her their hearts—we pray to the Lord. That her legacy of integrity and excellence will inspire generations to come to pursue the vision she shared with John Kennedy—of America as "a city upon a hill."

Father Modrys spoke of the wisdom of America's tolerance and celebration of diversity among many groups of people. "Though we can not wipe away all our tears, let them be tears of hope and not of despair. The fulfillment of this pledge—all the evidence suggests—is far in the future. Yet the miracle, we believe, has begun."

No matter what happened in the past, Americans sense that a better world was defined by President Kennedy's idealism. Judith Jamison's testimony recalls her feelings when she heard the news about President Kennedy in November 1963: "And I heard the bells tolling in Philadelphia and I didn't know what had happened. And when I found out, then I was devastated. Where once there was light in the hollow of your heart, it wasn't there anymore. It felt as if a kind of vacuum opened that creates extraordinary art. That kind of emptiness creates extraordinary generosity in anyone who's in a creative field. You feel that, you gotta fill that space. You gotta fill that light."

Caroline chose to read a poem from a book that her mother kept on a special bookshelf in her room. The selection suggests that maybe Caroline has asked herself the question, "Why didn't she ever write a book?" It was always clear that after winning a national award from *Vogue* for her writing, not fashion, Jackie possessed the talent to write. She was once on that path, the path to becoming a writer, but chose to give that gift to others as a book editor. Caroline points out, "In the frontispiece of the book reads: The Maria McKinney Memorial Award in Literature, First Prize presented to Jacqueline Bouvier, June 1946. And the poem is called 'Memory of Cape Cod' by Edna St. Vincent Millay."

> *The wind in the ash-tree sounds like the surf on the*
> *shore at Truro.*
> *I will shut my eyes . . . hush, be still with your*
> *silly bleating, sheep on Shillingstone Hill . . .*
> *They said: Leave your pebbles on the sand, and your*
> *shells, too, and come along, we'll find you another*
> *beach like the beach at Truro.*

Jessye Norman sang the communion song: "Ave Maria" by Franz Schubert and the prayer "Hail Mary". In Hyannisport, Boston and America's matriarch, Rose Fitzgerald Kennedy celebrated her one hundred and fourth birthday. She lived past the death of her husband, Joe, her sons Joe, Jr., Jack, Bobby, her daughter "Kick', her grand-son David, and now her daughter-in-law, Jackie. The Kennedy's political beliefs may best be understood through their deeply religious mother's love and faith in her family.

Senator Kennedy rose to give the eulogy. The Senator's Boston "r's" sounded like Jack's voice. "No one ever gave more meaning to the title of First Lady. The nation's capital city looks as it does because of her. She saved Lafayette Square and Pennsylvania Avenue. Jackie brought the greatest artist to the White House," the memory of Pablo Casals, Igor Stravinsky, Isaac Stern, Leonard Bernstein, Grace Bumbry and Jackie applauding Brazil's lyrical *bossa nova* create a visual montage of 20th century artistic excellence, " . . . and the arts to the center of national attention. Today, in large part because of her inspiration and vision, the arts are an abiding part of national policy. President Kennedy took such delight in her brilliance and her spirit. At a White House dinner, he once leaned over and told the French Ambassador's wife, Madelaine Malraux, "Jackie speaks fluent French. But I only understand one out of every five words she says—and that word is De Gaulle." Her beauty and manners are well-documented, but a rare ability to pass on the gifts she was blessed with to others, is the gift that brings us closer to knowing her.

Senator Kennedy spoke of Jackie's gifts to her extended family, and how Robert F. Kennedy sustained her as they shared hopes to carry on Jack's vision. Of her children, he said, "They are her two miracles." On fame: "She never wanted public notice—in part, I think, because it brought back painful memories of an unbearable sorrow, endured in the glare of a million lights . . . she made a rare and noble contribution to the American spirit . . . may the angels take you into paradise . . . may the martyrs come to welcome you on your way, and lead you into the holy city, Jerusalem . . ."

At Arlington National Cemetery, President Kennedy's eternal flame, like a nocturnal spirit, guards the Lee Mansion's majestic hilltop scene, with aerial views of the Lincoln, Jefferson and Washington memorials. It is a glamourous view of the world worthy of great American heroes and heroines. The weary group of mourners circled President Kennedy's memorial grave at Jackie's funeral. A path, on the slope of the hill, leads to Robert Kennedy's grave. Along the patio, engraved on a stone wall are the words of his favorite poet Aeschylus. These are the words that Bobby lived by " . . . and even in our sleep, pain that cannot forget, falls drop by drop upon the heart, and in our own despair, against our will, comes wisdom to us by the awful grace of God."

When Jackie married the divorced Greek Orthodox Aristotle Onassis, the Vatican's notorious opposition of the marriage proclaimed the Roman Rota religious laws did not sanction a Roman Catholic marriage to a divorced person. In the past any Catholic who divorced and remarried was automatically excommunicated. Jackie, an American Catholic, was declared 'a public sinner' and the Church's supreme marriage tribunal investigated the 'irregular position' of her marriage. Undeterred, Jackie and 'Aristo' traveled like royalty to tour Egyptian archaeology. They cruised the Greek archipelago in the Ionian Sea, exploring his favorite island Ithaka. Whether on Skorpios or the *Christina*, for a little more than fifteen minutes on Andy Warhol's time, Onassis was a spectacular king of the sea. Mystified by Greek mythology, he reveled in all the pleasures life holds for big dreamers, and modeled his success on Ulysses, the hero of Homer's *Odyssey*. In Nikos Kazantzakis' *The Odysseus: A Modern Sequel*, an epic poem that continues the story of Homer where the *Odyssey* ends, he describes Greece "the sun like a night lamp transformed the sea into an iridescent cloth of mother-of-pearl . . . a magical portal opened and conducted me into an astonishing world."

On March 15, 1975, Aristotle Onassis died in Paris. The Vatican 'dropped' the Kennedy-Onassis investigation, reforming the Roman Rota religious laws so Catholics may marry divorced people. Two generations of the Onassis family, including Ari, his beloved sisters Artemis, Merope and Kalliroi, and his daughter Christina have died. The family grave on Skorpios near the tiny chapel of Panayista, "Little Virgin", is haunted by the unexpected death of Alexander Onassis, his only son. For Ari, these words ring true, "though we can not wipe away all our tears, let them be tears of hope and not of despair."

At the burial ceremony, Jacqueline Bouvier Kennedy Onassis was carved on the headstone. The Cape Cod sea, walks along the sandy shore, an Aegean breeze and the tousled memories of Jackie and JFK sipping New England clam chowder on board the *Honey Fitz* are the images of her life. Whether sailing off the coast of Martha's Vineyard on Maurice Tempelsman's yacht the *Relemar* or taking an afternoon swim near the anquored *Christina*, the mystery of the open sea frames the history of her life.

The Most Reverend Philip M. Hannan gave the final benediction, "In the ancient cemeteries of the Christians, called catacombs, the inscriptions on the tombs showed their beliefs . . . O God, the author of the unbought grace of life, you are our promised home. Jacqueline . . . with the presence of your everlasting life and love . . . there to join the other members of her family . . ." Jackie, a Catholic, believes that there is a place in God's kingdom where all your earthly troubles have vanished, your spirit soars into heaven, to a 'city upon a hill'. The United States Navy Sea Chanters offered a simple prayer, "O hear us when we cry to thee, For those in peril on the sea . . ."

In 1963, at President Kennedy's funeral the Most Reverend Philip M. Hannan, Auxiliary Bishop of Washington recited a long passage from President Kennedy's inaugural speech, "Let both sides unite to heed in all corners of the Earth the command of Isaiah— 'to undo the heavy burdens . . . and let the oppressed go free.' " Thirty years later, Jackie recaptured her husband's passion for Isaiah's ancient promise in her funeral mass.

After her death for many weeks, a flurry of memorials appeared around Manhattan. The Municipal Art Society placed a book of remembrance in Grand Central's restored waiting room, attracting a long line of commuters waiting to leave a token of thanks. Carly Simon, the reticent singer, gave a mid-afternoon concert in Grand Central to honor Jackie's great battle to preserve the train station. Mrs. Jayne B. Wrightsman, a devoted mentor to the former First Lady, offered The Metropolitan Museum of Art a portrait painting by Pierre Paul Prud'hon, *Talleyrand, Grand Chamberlain*. Charles-Maurice de Talleyrand-Perigord (1754-1838) served as Napoleon's effective Minister of Foreign Affairs, and was admired by both President Kennedy and Jackie. The Mayor of New York City, Rudolph Guiliani rededicated the Central Park Reservoir as the Jacqueline Kennedy Onassis Reservoir, an homage to her deep devotion to preserve the loveliness of the city's finest public garden. American Ballet Theatre, The New York City Ballet, Dance Theater of Harlem, and many other cultural organizations acknowledged her patronage.

"The goal is to live with godlike composure on the full rush of energy, like Dionysus riding the tiger, without being torn to pieces," believes Joseph Campbell. Jackie, as if a Dionysian paragon, gave to herself the greatest memorial of all, by living a passionate life. Campbell forewarns that, "there is no security in following the call to adventure." In a miraculous way, her fame permitted strangers to voyage into her world of artists, painters, poets and kings. As if her whole life were on stage, the world loved to watch her pageant go by.

JACKIE ON THE EVE OF THE ELECTION

Jackie's private life burst into the national limelight in 1960. A dutiful politician's wife, she joined Senator Kennedy's crisscross presidential campaign across America. Americans stared, and wondered if she might be the *one*, our new first lady. Reporters began to examine her clothes, were they too fancy, was she too chic? Who are the Kennedy's? When her doctors advised that a pregnant woman should not be campaigning, she stayed home and supported his efforts with radio and television interviews and wrote a nationally syndicated column *Campaign Wife*.

In November of 1960, Jackie's interview finale elevated her image into public adoration after the four televised Nixon-Kennedy debates scheduled on September 26th, October 7th, October 13th and October 21st. The plan called for Henry Fonda to interview Mrs. John F. Kennedy on November 2nd so the national press could get the women's perspective on politics, and Kennedy could secure the women's vote. Henry Fonda described the program before the national audience: "Mrs. Kennedy told me we're going to see some movies of the family and look at a few pages of the Kennedy family album. Later Mrs. Kennedy will be asking the Senator about those issues in the election that women all over the country have told her are the most important to them."

"I feel like a boxer going into Madison Square Garden," Jack Kennedy said to Dave Powers minutes before the Nixon-Kennedy debates. The press and the public considered Vice President Nixon the probable winner of the election contest before seventy-million Americans. When they were over, the positions of the two contestants were reversed. Kennedy's quick witted, electric persona on the television cameras had stirred a nation fascinated with the 'star quality' of American movie idols.

Khrushchev the leader of the Communist world and Castro arrived in New York City for the opening of the United Nations' General Assembly. Manhattan turned into a military state with armed police guards stationed at all the Iron Curtain consulates. Khrushchev's arrival was perfectly timed with the first three Nixon-Kennedy debates. His mission, tormenting the United Nations with his usual world domineering rhetoric, ended as Nixon seemed to be perspiring in the heat of competition. His televised farewell to America and the United Nations on October 13th showed Mr. Khrushchev pounding his shoe in anger on the table declaring that, "History is on our side."

On September 29, 1960 in Syracuse, New York, after the first debate, the energy on the campaign trail gathered a new momentum and a hopeful, Senator John F. Kennedy spoke about the threats posed by the Soviet Union: "The reason is that Mr. Khrushchev is not the enemy. He may personify it. But the real enemy is the Communist system itself, unyielding in its drive for world domination. We must summon the strength of this Nation and the free world to advance the cause of peace."

In early November, Kennedy arrived in San Francisco and then journeyed to Los Angeles. In Los Angeles on November 2nd, CBS was scheduled to nationally broadcast Henry Fonda in New York City interviewing Mrs. John F. Kennedy in Washington D.C. Then she would interview her husband, Senator Kennedy on her campaign efforts with women around the country.

"And now, Mr. Fonda," on national television, Mrs. Kennedy greeted her friend, "Hello, Mr. Fonda. You're very nice to take the time to be with us today!"

Henry Fonda concedes, "Oh, this is my pleasure. What about your scrapbook and the movies?"

Sharing her private 'family album' on national television was bizarrely out of character for Jacqueline Kennedy. She replies, "It's really a little bit of everything. Some photographs and film, many of which I've taken myself over the past seven years. I thought people might enjoy seeing them."

Privacy to Jackie was not only a public fear of being hounded by reporters, but a very personal one as well. In a quiet moment during a family dinner conversation, Jack Kennedy once turned to his wife and said, "A penny for your thoughts?" Jackie answered, "But they're my thoughts Jack, and they wouldn't be my thoughts anymore if I told them. Now would they?" The Kennedy brothers and sisters laughed, and Joe Kennedy said, "I like a girl with a mind of her own, a girl like us."

Henry Fonda asks the Senator's wife, "Did you ever imagine when you were married what was going to be happening now?"

Mrs. Kennedy laughs, "No, I never did. We were married in September 1953 and in those seven years so much has happened. Jack was in his first term in the Senate then."

Henry Fonda asks, "Oh, that's your Washington home. How beautiful. It's a wonderful example of Federal architecture. Did you ever find out how old it is?"

"No, it's ancient. I know it's just old enough for Jack. He loves old things." Jackie admired her husband's sense of history, and once remarked, "When you read Proust, or listen to Jack talk about history or go to Mount Vernon, you understand. I feel so strongly about the children who come to the White House. When I think about my own son, and how to make him turn out like his father, I think of Jack's great sense of history."

Mrs. Kennedy says, "And here we are reading." The Kennedy family invented their own special meanings for words, fantastic is used to underscore family approval. The moment Jack told her she was 'the one,' Jackie was hailed as the Kennedy family's most 'fantastic reader'.

Janet Lee Bouvier Auchincloss, influenced her daughters, Jackie and Lee, to appreciate art, poetry and painting as young children.

"When I was a child my mother helped us enormously with our creative instincts . . . she encouraged us to make things for her birthday present instead of buying them. So perhaps we would paint a picture or write a poem or memorize something. When I was ten years old, I memorized 'The Vision of Sir Launfal' by James Russel Lowell for my mother's birthday. It was eleven pages long in my poetry book. I remember how proud I was of myself."

It was Janet Auchincloss who discovered the entry form for *Vogue* magazine's *Prix de Paris* writing competition that catapulted her daughter's first glorious national victory as a writer.

Henry Fonda inquires, "I don't imagine the Senator does much reading these days."

Jackie's sense of humor is provoked, "He's too busy talking, but his idea of a perfect evening still is to stay home and read. Before we were married, whenever he gave me a present it was usually a book. History. Biography . . . there's Caroline Bouvier Kennedy—age eighteen months."

Jackie once described Jack Kennedy's style of dating: "He was not the candy-and-flowers type, so every now and then he gave me a book. *The Raven*, which is the life of Sam Houston, and also *Pilgrim's Way* by John Buchan."

Henry Fonda, "I know you were more interested in writing once!"

Mrs. Kennedy, "That's right. When I first met Jack, about a year before we were married, I was working for the *Washington Times Herald*. I was their Inquiring Photographer."

Henry Fonda jokingly pries into her love life, "I heard you met the Senator in the line of duty?"

Jackie makes a quick recovery, "That's a marvelous story but I can't fool you. I met him at the home of our friends the Bartletts' in Georgetown who were earnestly matchmaking and for once it worked . . ."

A serious Henry Fonda probes Jackie's philanthropic activities: "And what's this?"

"A Washington foundling home. I spend some of my days

there regularly. Jack's family has a strong commitment to children's charities, so after I was married I became very interested in that work too . . . Quick lunch in a drug store on my way to hear Jack speak in the Senate." The camera tracks Jackie on her way to Congress.

"Don't tell me you're the kind of wife who goes to her husband's office a lot?" Henry Fonda espouses the 1950's pre-feminist male sympathy for any women who is burdened with two professions, mother and career. Yet, Jackie gracefully performs both her roles as an effective *Campaign Wife* and a doting mother.

Her engaging enthusiasm proves this assignment may be a favorite: "I did do some research there for some of his Senate speeches and at home. The speech on Indochina, because so much of the source material was in French. I did the same for his Algerian speech."

Jackie referenced the Algerian speech because Senator Kennedy served on the Foreign Relations Committee in the Senate and ardently opposed French colonialism in Algeria. Kennedy had studied the geography of Communism and concluded that there were six key areas around the world, where, "we are reacting too late to a cold war crisis where the cause of freedom is in serious trouble." The key countries were *Cuba, Ghana, Japan,* the area once known as *Indochina,* where the tiny nation of Laos struggled to maintain independence, *Poland,* where the once hopeful cracks in the Iron Curtain seem to be gradually disappearing, and *India.* Kennedy pointed out, "India, the one nation capable of surpassing China for the economic leadership of the Asian continent, is meeting one set back after another."

Henry Fonda wonders, "Did you discuss the Algerian speech when you met General de Gaulle?" Mrs. Kennedy, "No, I would leave that up to Jack. But I often translate for him."

Although her political interests were primarily to advance her husband's causes, she aided Senator Kennedy in a unique way. On a visit to Rome in 1955, the American Ambassador Clare Booth Luce invited Jack and Jackie to dine at the United States Embassy with the former French Prime Minister, Georges Bidault. After dinner, the men wished to have a private discussion, but Kennedy and Bidault did not share a common language. Jackie gave a command performance acting as the two foreigners interpreter. Bidault later wrote to her, "I have never seen so much wisdom adorned with so much charm."

The Kennedy's political strategies must be analyzed in terms of their ability to persuade the press to admire them and even join their efforts. Henry Fonda's television program with Jackie was pure entertainment. Her charming manners, graceful intelligence, and her darling baby Caroline, aroused a formidable admiration for the Kennedy family as a model American family. The distinguished Joseph W. Alsop, the FDR insider journalist at the *Herald Tribune* whose mother was a first cousin of Eleanor Roosevelt's, wrote in his memoirs, *I've Seen the Best of It:* "By the time of John Kennedy's reelection to the Senate in 1958, I had concluded that he was the most likely Democrat nominee for the 1960 election and resolved to help him in any way to win the presidency... Kennedy's viewpoints on foreign and domestic policy were essentially identical with my own, always an endearing trait in any presidential candidate, and I was convinced that he had a strong chance to win the general election..."

Jackie confides to Fonda, "I haven't been able to do much really because I'm expecting the baby. But since we've been married I've campaigned with him in forty-six states and I traveled with him in the primaries early this year but I couldn't go to the convention."

At the 1960 Democratic National Convention, Judy Garland, the most famous Dorothy in America, who sang 'Somewhere Over the Rainbow', was an honored guest, seated next to Senator Kennedy. In *The Wizard of Oz*, Dorothy's nightmare crash-landed her in the middle of a foreign country Munchinland. Terrified of never seeing her loved ones again, she searched in vain for someone to help her find her way back home. In the end, she discovers she possessed the power to make her dream come true. Along the way, she accidentally conquered evil, the wicked *Witch of the West*, and transformed her new friends by helping them get a *brain*, a *heart* and a *medal of courage*. Dorothy's legacy is the quintessential American fairytale about awakening people's inner goodness and honorable intentions. She whispers, "It's a powerful thing to believe." With the innocence of a child's determination, she gave hope to the sad lives of three lost souls, and her dreamy idealism captured the Kennedy's imagination. At the convention, Jack Kennedy made no false claims: "The New Frontier of which I speak is not a set of promises but a set of challenges . . ."

Jackie's campaign efforts play on television as she narrates the film: "Here are the press teas this fall . . . Meeting with *Women of the New Frontier*. And the ticker tape parade two weeks ago in New York."

Two of the Kennedy's most devoted friends, Dave Powers and Kenneth O'Donnell, once observed of the 1958 senatorial campaign in Massachusetts that, "when Jackie was traveling with us, the size of the crowds at every stop were twice as big as they would have been if Jack was traveling alone." Jackie fondly recalls, "I'm so glad Jack comes from Massachusetts because it is the state with the most history . . . we'd pass John Quincy Adams house or Harvard or Plymouth . . . we stayed in Boston on election night and Jack won by an incredible majority . . . we were so happy!"

Fonda is now completely charmed by Jackie, totally impressed with her spirited campaign efforts, a devoted fan, "I know all about this, your triumph—your speech in Italian on Columbus Day in New York and in Spanish to the Puerto Ricans. And now a surprise. You've shown us some of your movies, now we want to show you some of ours. I call this: "The Triumph of Jacqueline Kennedy, or My Favorite Linguist."

A film runs capturing a pregnant Jacqueline Kennedy campaigning in Italian and Spanish.

Mrs. Kennedy rejoices, "Prego, Signore Fonda!"

While Jackie campaigned in New York, Julie Andrews prepared to play Queen Guinevere in the medieval Broadway musical

Camelot. Alan Jay Lerner, an old Choate schoolmate of Jack's, the stage director Moss Hart, and composer Frederick Loewe, struggled with mounting difficulties to stage the spectacular adaptation of T.H. White's novel *The Once and Future King.* Richard Burton as King Arthur, Julie Andrews as his Queen and Robert Goulet as her tragic lover Lancelot rehearsed for the upcoming opening night in mid-December of 1960.

A delighted Henry Fonda is impressed with Jackie's activities, "Mrs. Kennedy, besides traveling with the Senator, and press teas, and "Women of the New Frontier," what about your *Calling for Kennedy* drives?"

Jackie's voice lights up because the *Calling for Kennedy* campaign distinguished her efforts in the national arena. "I felt it was important to find out what issues in this election are of the most significance to women around the country. And those are the things I want to talk to Jack about. That's why *Calling for Kennedy* was organized."

The *Calling for Kennedy* film begins with Jackie gracefully thanking, " . . . all of you for *being there* . . . for assembling so many people to start out *Calling for Kennedy* week, which helps finances anew, and I know you'll go into the homes of all these women and find out the issues which concern them the most, which I will report to my husband."

Mrs. Kennedy explains how the results were evaluated, "Everywhere, peace is uppermost in women's minds. They say that if we can't keep the peace, then the other issues aren't important. Not one women called upon, put the budget ahead of peace."

Suddenly Fonda is signaled that California has Senator Kennedy linked to the broadcast. He announces Jack, "Mrs. Kennedy, they tell me they have Senator Kennedy in Los Angeles now.

Senator Kennedy starts in with, "Hello, Jackie. Hello, Mr. Fonda."

Mrs. Kennedy, "Hello, Jack. How is it in California?"

Senator Kennedy, "Well, we've had a very good trip out here. Going to leave again tonight. We travel in sixteen states in the next seven days, then come back to Massachusetts on Monday night. We'll meet you and Caroline on Tuesday morning, when all this long running around the country comes to an end on election day, November 8th. I must say I'll be glad when it does finally come to an end. I'll be glad to see you both."

Jackie explains the results of her work to her husband, "Hundreds of the *Calling for Kennedy* forms have come in. And I know women around the country are anxious to have you know how they feel. Almost without exception, every form lists peace as the most important issue . . . we need a foreign policy which has foresight, not crisis-to-crisis planning."

Senator Kennedy replies, "Well, I think it is the great issue that we all face as Americans in 1960's. How can we keep the peace, and how can we protect our security? And I must say that, after having been through World War II, and then, of course, losing my older brother Joe, I don't think anyone wants to see that happen again. So, if I'm elected President, we're going to work with all our energies, all of our effort, to maintain the peace. I think we're going to have to do better than we're now doing . . . I've been talking a good deal in this campaign about national prestige, what people think of us abroad. That isn't the question of whether we're popular or not. What it does mean is whether people will follow us, whether the free world will accept our leadership, whether they will stand with us."

Mrs. Kennedy discusses the next issue concerning women, "Second in importance, judging from these, is the problem of educating our children . . . tax resources of the Federal Government should be made available to our educational system. A number of women have asked for Federal Aid for college scholarships. I know you have strong feelings about these issues."

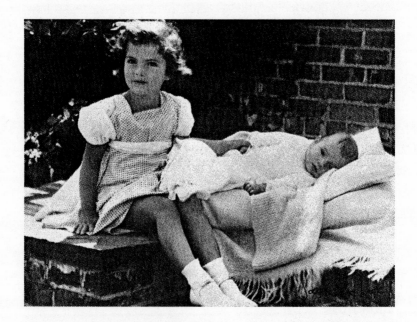

Senator Kennedy: "Well, I believe that education is funda-mental and basic. I come from a section of the United States which started the first public school . . . Ten years ago, we turned out twice as many scientists and engineers as the Russians, now they turn out twice as many as we do. I want everyone who has talent and wants to learn to have that chance. I want the United States to have the best-educated citizens in the world. That's the way we maintain democracy; that's the way we keep our freedom; that's the way we meet our responsibilities."

Mrs. Kennedy: "Another issue which affects almost every fam-ily is medical care for the aged. Many of the comments reveal that mothers of families are torn between the financial demands of edu-cating their children and meeting the medical bills of their aging parents."

Senator Kennedy: "Well, that problem is shared by a great many millions of Americans. The average social security check for sixteen million Americans over the age of sixty-five is about $72.00 a month. We suggest that medical care be tied to social security, every working American contribute, and it's little less than three cents a day during their working years . . . Unfortunately the bill which was passed and signed by the President provides that, be-fore any older person can get medical care, they have to exhaust their savings, and sign a petition, a "pauper's oath", and their chil-dren would have to do that too, exhaust their savings, which might represent all they had, before they could go down and get public assistance."

Mrs. Kennedy: "Before we finish, Jack, I still want to speak about peace again and how important it is to the women of this country . . . we must have peace at all costs, except, of course, at the cost of freedom. I agree, and I also feel very strongly that we must set a good example of democracy at home if we are to be the leaders of the free world and enjoy the friendship and respect of the people. Many women are concerned with the failure of disar-mament negotiations . . . can't we accomplish something concrete about disarmament?"

Senator Kennedy: "Well, it is, of course Jackie, the great problem. And I don't think we've made enough progress, for example, in the area of disarmament in the last years. We've only had about one hundred people working in the entire Federal Government on the subject of disarmament, the subject of nuclear testing. That's a terribly important subject. It involves the lives and security of us all. I believe we should set up an arms research institute—a peace institute—in the National Government, which will work as hard on the subject of disarmament, work as hard on the subject of peace, as our Defense Establishment does to protect us. Secondly, we ought to try to recognize that these are very changing times in the world. Eight years ago, there was no outer space, and now the Soviets have beaten us to outer space. We're going to have to do better there."

Kennedy added, "I've seen enough of war and so has America, to know that peace is our objective. The Bible said, 'Blessed are the peacemakers,' and that's what we must be in the 1960's."

Mrs. Kennedy: "Thank you, Jack. When will we see you again?"

Senator Kennedy: "Well, in one week. I'll look forward to being home. So I will see you on Tuesday. In the meanwhile, as I said, I'll be going into seventeen states, so we'll be working all the time. But we'll see you both Tuesday, November 8th, which is Election Day, and which is for me, the end of the trail. It may be the beginning, but we'll have to wait and see."

Mrs. Kennedy: "Goodbye, Jack . . . I want to thank the many thousands of women volunteers who have helped in the campaign . . . Goodbye, Mr. Fonda, and thank you for taking the time to visit with us here today."

Mr. Fonda: "Goodbye, Senator, Goodbye Mrs. Kennedy. I hope you enjoyed being with the Kennedy's as much as I did—Caroline's kittens and all the rest of it. I think they're a fine family, but I'm pretty partial. Good afternoon."

The interview was a great success, and Jackie's performance was perfectly directed by Henry Fonda's camaraderie. November 8th was just six days away. Jackie rested in Hyannisport as the

Senator and his remarkable team, famously nicknamed "the brain trust", Ted Sorenson, Richard Goodwin and Mike Feldman, tirelessly campaigned. Journalist Theodore White traveled with the Kennedy entourage, documenting the election strategies for his history book *The Making of the President.*

"We're being clobbered," said Bobby on election day. At 7:15 as if to confirm Bobby's dismay came a televised report that the IBM computers had just quoted odds on Nixon's victory at 100 to 1. Jack declared, "that machine is crazy!" and lit one of his favorite cigars a Havana Royal panatela. The Kennedy sisters gleefully danced about the compound as if at a party. Caroline Kennedy requested her father to kiss her goodnight. The little girl had a scratch on her nose and wanted him to see it. After his daughter was satisfied with his inspection and goodnight kisses, he joined Jackie and Bill Walton for a Daiquiri and a relaxing discussion about his painting abilities.

Ted Sorenson arrived to watch the election results. Pierre Salinger, Kennedy's press chief, scolded the Kennedy sisters for leaking to the press that Jack was already "smoking a big, black cigar" and "jumping up and down for joy!" It was reported on national television, and the election votes had not been fully tallied. Around 10:30, a landslide seemed inevitable and Jackie turned to her husband and said, "Oh, Bunny you're president now!" Jack replied a sobering, "No . . . no . . . it's too early yet." At 11:30, Jackie who was three weeks away from giving birth went upstairs to bed, and Jack Kennedy joined Ted Sorenson, Pierre Salinger and Bobby in the communications center (Bobby's house).

In the December 19th issue of *Life* magazine journalist, Hugh Sidney, interviews Joseph P. Kennedy on the election results: "I didn't think it would be that close. I was wrong on two things. First, I thought he would get a bigger Catholic vote than he did. Second, I did not think so many would vote against him because of his religion." The final vote tabulates Kennedy with 303 electoral votes from twenty-three states and Nixon with 219 from twenty-six states. Kennedy lost California, Nixon's home state.

In the same issue of *Life*, the cover story was the christening of John F. Kennedy, Jr. Just one month old and already he was front page news. Dressed in his father's baptismal gown, the new baby was attended by his godmother Mrs. Charles Bartlett. Jackie's sister Lee, divorced but now happily remarried to Poland's Communist exiled royalty lived with her husband Prince Stanislas Radziwill in London. Since the couple could not attend the ceremony, Charles Bartlett stood in as proxy godfather for Prince Radziwill at Georgetown University's chapel.

At John, Jr.'s baptismal ceremony, the Irish Ambassador, Thomas Kiernan, presented the Kennedy's with a Wexford Cup to celebrate the arrival of a new baby and the presidency.

Jackie and especially President Kennedy were deeply moved when Irish poet D. L. Kelleher's poem was dedicated to the new baby:

> We wish to the new child
> A heart that can be beguiled by a flower
> That the wind lifts as it passes
> Over the grasses after a summer shower
> A heart that can recognize
> The gifts that life holds for the wise
> When the storms break for him
> May the trees shake for him their blossoms down
> In the night that he is troubled
> May a friend wake for him
> So that his time be doubled
> And at the end of all loving and love
> May the Man above
> Give him a crown

On January 20th, the 35th President of the United States John F. Kennedy was sworn into office. In his inauguration speech he states: "To those people in huts and villages of half the globe struggling to break the bonds of mass misery, we pledge our best efforts to help them help themselves . . . if a free society cannot help the many who are poor, it can not save the few who are rich. To our sister republics south of the border, we offer a special pledge, to convert our good words into good deeds, to assist free people in casting off the chains of poverty . . . But this peaceful revolution of hope cannot become the prey of hostile powers . . . And let every other power know that this hemisphere intends to remain the master of its own house . . . Let both sides seek to invoke the wonders of science instead of its terrors. Together let us explore the stars, conquer the deserts, eradicate disease, tap the ocean depths, and encourage the arts and commerce.."

Marian Anderson sang the *Star Spangled Banner* and Robert Frost wrote a poem:

> *The glory of the next Augustan age*
> *Of a power leading from its strength and pride*
> *Of young ambition eager to be tried*
> *Firm in our free beliefs without dismay*
> *In any game the nations want to play*
> *A Golden Age of poetry and power*
> *Of which this noonday's the beginning hour . . .*

The huge crystal white snowstorm in Washington D.C. delayed the arrival of some of the Inaugural Gala performances, adding an informal suspense and a glow of romance to the Kennedy's New Frontier.

Frank Sinatra's daughter Nancy remembers the evening's impact on her father: "the inaugural celebration was a milestone event for my father . . . for the son of an immigrant Italian couple who had risen from the streets of Hoboken to become the biggest and most powerful star in show business, it was a moment to savor for a lifetime." Sinatra instructed the orchestra to play *My Fair Lady's* '*I Could Have Danced All Night*', when the ingenue First Lady entered the Inaugural Gala ballroom:

I could have spread my wings
And done a thousand things
I've never done before
I'll never know what made it so exciting
Why all at once my heart took flight
I only know when he began to dance with me
I could have danced, danced, danced all night . . .

Sinatra not only organized the entertainment for the Inaugural Ball, but when he discovered that Ethel Merman and Sir Laurence Olivier could not be released from Broadway performances, he bought out the house and shut down the theater for the night. Frank Sinatra set the hour when America watched Washington with astonished eyes. The performers: Ella Fitzgerald, Joey Bishop, Nat King Cole, Jimmy Durante, Harry Belafonte, Ethel Merman, Sir Laurence Olivier, Helen Traubel, Leonard Bernstein and Bette Davis gave the audience a spectacular show.

CULTURAL EXCHANGE: A KENNEDY MISSION

On September 29, 1960, Charles Collingwood interviewed the candidate's wife regarding her official duties as a potential first lady: "She will have an official role . . . in my case it would be education, helping children, student and cultural exchange programs . . ."

Jack and Jackie Kennedy immediately embarked on a full scale effort to build a prestigious national image by entertaining the best musicians, composers, novelists and focus on celebrating the culture of America's diverse ethnic background. President Kennedy signed the Mutual Education and Cultural Exchange Act on September 21, 1961. A few months later in December, President Kennedy and Jacqueline traveled to Latin America to announce a broad program of investments, The Alliance for Progress, to improve local housing, fund industrial growth and advance the cause of freedom in Puerto Rico, Columbia, and Venezuela. President Kennedy announced his wife in Venezuela: "Ladies and gentleman, one of the Kennedy's does not need an interpreter. So, I'd like to have my wife say a word or two." The first lady spoke in the native language, blessing the audience with a plea that if they supported her husband's relief programs she was sure they would benefit. Her few words inspired an unforgettable affection.

A few months before the journey to Latin America, Jackie was championing the idea of inviting Pablo Casals to perform at the White House. Pablo Casals, in protest of American support of Spain's dictator Generalissimo Franco, had, in the past fifty years, refused to perform at the White House. President and Jacqueline Kennedy wrote this letter to Pablo Casals dated October 10, 1961: " Mrs. Kennedy and I would like to extend an invitation to you to give a concert at The White House on Monday evening, November 13th. We feel that your performance as one of the world's great artists would lend distinction to the entertainment of our invited guests."

Isaac Stern, an effective advisor on Kennedy's Presidential Advisory Council on the Arts, and a close friend of Casals remembers that time fondly: "I met Casals in 1950 when I performed in the first Casals Festival and the three subsequent ones in Puerto Rico. Casals was invited to The White House to perform with Alexander Schneider who created the Casals Festival and pianist Mieczyslaw Horszowski." The dinner and concert to honor Governor Munoz Marin of Puerto Rico was a landmark event because the Kennedy's invited America's most prominent contemporary composers and conductors: Samuel Barber, Norman Dello Joio, Walter Piston, Alan Hovhaness, Gian Carlo Menotti, Roger H. Sessions, Virgil Thomson, Leonard Bernstein, Eugene Ormandy and Leopold Stokowski. Isaac Stern describes his impressions: "I was there and that was an occasion to meet the President and Mrs. Kennedy and have some conversation . . . the musicianship had to do with artistic communication which both President Kennedy and Jackie Kennedy appreciated. It set an example of graciousness on having serious, serious artists at dinner and a recognition of where the arts belonged."

The Pablo Casals performance was one of the most celebrated concerts during the Kennedy years. As President Kennedy wished the cultural alliance between America and the Spanish speaking countries was strengthened, inspiring a deeper respect for the people's determination in those countries. While Pablo Casals shaped classical music with distinction, there was another Latin cultural phenomenon the *bossa nova*, which soared across America becoming an international hit. It all started with jazz guitarist, Charlie Byrd's State Department journey to Latin America in early

1961 to record the local musicians in Brazil. The trip was one of many cultural exchange programs developed under Edward R. Murrow's guidance of the United States Information Agency (USIA). The First Lady was so impressed with the *bossa nova,* she celebrated the lyrical Brazilian music at a White House concert.

In the early planning of the White House cultural exchange programs, Jacqueline Kennedy developed a performing arts series for young adults to mirror the dinners and concerts held to honor visiting heads of state. It was her way to connect children from all over the country to an international stage for music and the arts in a memorable setting the White House. The First Lady installed herself as a national spokesperson for children's early education of the performing arts. Her long time friend, Isaac Stern observes: "kids are naturally artistic. They dance, they sing, they paint, they draw, they are instinctively artistic. And you touch a child with the arts this way and suddenly you flower a possibly very decent human being. And Jackie Kennedy understood this because she believed in these things. We recognize when it's coming from the inside or when it's being prepared. For Jackie Kennedy, this was always from the inside. These are things she truthfully believed and she knew about them."

Charlie Byrd admired the way Jacqueline Kennedy inspired a greater appreciation of music, encouraging American culture to synthesize the influences of other nations indigenous music, mythology and folklore. Byrd's Kennedy State Department journey to Brazil to record the sounds of the *bossa nova* followed in the wake of the foreign film *Black Orpheus* winning an Academy Award in 1959. When Byrd returned in 1961, he invited legendary tenor saxophonist, Stan Getz, to record the album *Jazz Samba* in Pierce Hall, All Souls Unitarian Church in Washington D.C. on February 13th, 1962. Charlie Byrd and Stan Getz recorded Antonio Carlos Jobim's music from the tapes made in Brazil. In just a matter of weeks Antonio Carlos Jobim, and the Brazilian couple João and Astrud Gilberto would become the most famous Brazilians to set foot on American shores.

THE
STRATEGY
OF PEACE
BY
SENATOR JOHN F. KENNEDY
AUTHOR OF "PROFILES IN COURAGE"
EDITED BY ALLAN NEVINS

THE FOREIGN POLICY SPEECHES AND STATEMENTS ON DEFENSE, PEACE,
NATIONAL SECURITY AND RELATED DOMESTIC ISSUES OF A LEADING
PRESIDENTIAL CANDIDATE ARE HERE EDITED BY AN EMINENT HISTORIAN,
WHO HAS ALSO CONTRIBUTED AN INTRODUCTION. THE BOOK INCLUDES THE
SENATOR'S ANNOTATIONS AND AN INTERVIEW WITH HIM BY JOHN FISCHER.

$ .95

On November 19th, 1962, Mrs. Kennedy welcomed the fifth musical program for youth from Chicago. The Paul Winter Jazz Sextet played one of Antonio Carlos Jobim's *bossa nova* hits. The concert was held for sons and daughters of international ambassadors and chiefs of missions. By then, Astrud Gilberto's March 18th rendition of *The Girl From Ipanema* rose to the top of the jazz and pop charts and remains one of the great moments in music history. Astrud Gilberto was interviewed after her arrival in Washington D.C.: "I'm not a sociologist but it was a time when people in the States wanted to turn to something other than their troubles. There was a feeling of dissatisfaction—possibility the hint of war to come—and people needed some romance, something dreamy, for distraction. Americans are generally not very curious about the styles of other countries. The Beatles sang Rock & Roll in English, the common language—they were not really a foreign thing. Our music was Brazilian music in modern form. It was very pretty, and it was exceptional to so completely infiltrate the American music culture."

Charlie Byrd had no political awareness that in 1959, the Cuban dictator Fulgencio Bastista went out, ignomiously fleeing from Havana to the Dominican Republic. His place was usurped by Fidel Castro, a comparatively young attorney, who appeared to be a political enigma. Soon, he executed several of his enemies, and launched a revolutionary pro-Communist regime, with several high level government appointments. In early 1960, the United States government did not respond to counter-attack the cause for a true democracy in Cuba. Senator Kennedy responded by saying that, "Cuba is not an isolated case. We can still show our concern for liberty and our opposition to the status quo in our relations with other Latin-American dictators, who now, or in the future, try to suppress their people's aspirations."

After President Franklin Roosevelt visited Latin America in 1930, no other president went south of the border for thirty years, until President Kennedy and Jackie toured Puerto Rico, Columbia, Venezuela, Mexico and Costa Rica. On July 30, 1963 President

Kennedy hosted a special conference for Brazilian foreign exchange students. Charlie Byrd seemed unconcerned with the politics surrounding the Bay of Pigs, the Cuban Missile Crisis, or Kennedy's Alliance for Progress in Latin America. Rather Byrd, a cultural visionary, participated in one of the most successful infusions of another country's musical phenomenon, bringing to America the creators of the *bossa nova*; the composers Antonio Carlos Jobim and Luiz Bonfa, along with the singer João Gilberto.

In September of 1999, Charlie Byrd said, "My trio was selected for the USIA tour of Latin America, including Brazil. Our purpose was to show Americans doing their thing with music that they take very seriously. It was arranged for us to meet with many fine musicians along the way . . . including composer Antonio Carlos Jobim. By the end of the tour, this was the best received part of the program. I had not been thinking, "I've got a hit here," but I could tell that his music had a strong and wide appeal."

Byrd describes how he met Stan Getz "When we returned home, my wife Virginia and I had the occasion to hear Stan Getz in a small nightclub. It was she that said, "Wouldn't Stan sound great playing those Jobim tunes?" We invited Getz to come to our house for lunch the following day. I played him some tapes from the tour, and some things I had learned on the guitar. Stan liked the idea and arranged for us to make a recording for Verve Records produced by Creed Taylor. The rest is history, and Brazilian music has been a part of my repertoire ever since. I consider Antonio Carlos Jobim to be one of the most important composers of popular music in this century."

Charlie Byrd's personal history reflects the changing attitudes in the American jazz milieu. Just before the punch of the 1950's jazz movement, Byrd was dissatisfied with the lack of opportunities for jazz players, thus he moved forward with the idea of becoming a classical guitarist. Byrd's arrival in Washington D.C. and the Kennedy's State Department trip was perfect timing. The lyrical Brazilian music in the film *Black Orpheus* (Orfeu Negro) burst onto the screens of the United States and left the American viewer dazzled by the artistry of its creators. Americans were impressed by the natural beauty of Brazil and its people and wholly captivated by the relentlessly rhythmic music of Rio. *Black Orpheus* directed by Marcel Camus was awarded the Grand Prize at the Cannes Film Festival in 1959 and an Academy Award for Best Foreign Film. Antonio Carlos Jobim and Luiz Bonfa's *bossa nova* was internationally acclaimed.

Byrd was familiar with the music, and better still, as a classical guitarist, he knew how to play it beautifully. Lore has it that Byrd's interest in the *bossa nova* happened during the twelve week State Department tour of Brazil in 1961, but that is not true. Before the trip, an earlier recorded trio engagement at New York's Village Vanguard in January of that year found him edging toward the use of Brazilian rhythms in his music. Charlie says, "I don't know the exact date, but on one night, I invited Bola Sete to sit in, and I was suddenly aware of Brazil."

The Latin American tour immersed Charlie Byrd in Brazil's rapidly developing *bossa nova* movement. He returned to Washington D.C. transformed by Antonio Carlos Jobim's music, and included the *bossa nova* in his sets at the Showboat. After Stan Getz flipped over the new seductive sounds, he convinced Verve to make a *bossa nova* album with Byrd. *Jazz Samba*, led by a Jobim's *Desafinado* on the B-side of a 45 RPM single, became a runaway hit launching the *bossa nova* as an international force.

The first bossa nova hit in the United States, *Desafinada,* won a Grammy. *Jazz Samba* was followed one year later by the million-selling album *Getz/Gilberto* which won two Grammy awards. The popularity of João and Astrud Gilberto exploded with the romantic tune *The Girl From Ipanema*. Stan Getz recognized Jobim brought a new spiritual depth into the international jazz scene with an unusually formidable appeal. After the February 13th Pierce Hall recording, Getz organized the following 1962 recordings and performances: *Big Band Bossa Nova* on August 27 to 28th at Columbia 30th Street Studio in New York City, and *Getz/Gilberto* on March 18 to 19th at A&R Studios. The next year Stan Getz and

Charlie Byrd recorded *Jazz Samba Encore* on February 9, 1963 at
Webster Hall, followed by *Stan Getz/Laurindo* on March 22nd,
1963. Soon after, Antonio Carlos Jobim, Stan Getz, João Gilberto,
Astrud Gilberto departed for their 1963 tour in Europe.

Astrud Gilberto was an unwelcome addition to the *Getz/
Gilberto* album. Her husband João and Jobim objected she was
not a professional singer, just a housewife. But Stan Getz's wife,
Monica heard her sing, told her husband Astrud's voice is *The Girl
From Ipanema*. Monica and Stan Getz prevailed.

> *Soft and tender, young and lovely,*
> *The girl from Ipanema goes walking*
> *And when she passes, each one goes "Ai!"*
> *But when she walks its like a samba*
> *That swings so cool and sways so gently*
> *That when she passes, the one she passes goes, "Ai!"*

Astrud recalls, "I sang *The Girl From Ipanema* for Stan, and he
said, 'Yeah, that's fine with me.' I'd known him already a few
weeks. At the studio, after we listened to the finished take, Stan
looked at me and said very emphatically, 'That song is gonna make
you very famous.' I was not a professional musician. I thought the
song was beautiful, but I had no plans to follow it up. After the
recording, I went on a European tour with Stan and João for several months. Then we returned to the States on the day of President Kennedy's funeral." Many years later, Monica Getz observes,
"Jackie told me she loves the *bossa nova*, and still plays it at home."

Antonio Carlos Jobim, João and Astrud Gilberto's Brazilian
mythology is one of the most extraordinary examples of how the
Kennedy's fostered a formidable alliance with artists of a foreign
country. On January 30th, 1967, Frank Sinatra and Antonio Carlos
Jobim recorded an album together completing the American love
affair with the bossa nova. Sinatra described Jobim "as slight and
tousled boy-man, speaking softly while about him rushes a world

too fast. Antonio, troubled not by the clamor in the world, troubled more by the whisperings in his heart."

Jackie continued to admire both the cultures of Latin America and Spain. After her husband's death, she traveled to Mexico (her 1953 honeymoon destination with JFK), and toured Argentina with her children. In 1966 she appeared on the cover of *Life*. The headline *Jackie Kennedy, The Radiant Conquistadora* profiled Jackie dressed in the traditional Spanish equestrienne costume, *traje corto*. She graciously signed autographs and when asked to give a speech, she radiated appreciation for the warmth of her reception. For five days, she toured the architectural sights visiting the glorious former royal residence, Seville's Alcazar, and joined the Prince of Monaco and Princess, Grace Kelly to watch a flamenco dancer perform in a private *caseta*. On her unofficial goodwill visit, a Spanish diplomat commented, "The ties between our nations are better for her visit. The Spanish are always grateful to a beautiful woman." Once again Jackie immersed herself into the culture of a foreign country with grace, and an awe struck appreciation.

The USIA trip orchestrated the appreciation of a foreign musical sensation that no other administration has repeated. The Beatles came willingly, and Motown would soon become a national sensation. Isaac Stern remembers a national purpose in the arts, "The country needs that kind of mythology. Belief in beauty is a necessity. The White House led that. Jackie Kennedy above all believed in it. And oh, do we miss her."

APOTHEOSIS IN PARIS AND VIENNA

In 1963 Andre Malraux stated in New York City that: "It is essential that freedom not be defeated, and the world's writers of fiction are all too tempted by the most dangerous demons—. Culture is the free's world most powerful guardian against those demons . . . its most powerful ally in leading humanity to a dream worthy of man." Malraux's only living son Alain Malraux's impression of Jackie reflects his father's call for leadership in the artistic world, "She had a simple way of being a sovereign. The way she was welcoming new things, new artists, young painters, dancers, musicians as well. She was always opening her heart to art. Very few people in public life, in official life have this very friendly way to associate art to everyday life. She had it! "

Alain Malraux reminisced about spending Christmas and New Year's with Jackie at her Fifth Avenue apartment in 1968: "My mother was living at that time on Park Avenue. And I was going to visit her for Christmas. There was a long and extraordinary dinner Jacqueline gave, and she was not yet married to Onassis. Thanks to the big banker, Andre Meyer, we were invited, and it was a fantastic New Year's Eve. Everybody was given a marvelous gift, a Mahler recording by Lenny Bernstein."

Alain observed that his step-father, Andre Malraux, and Jackie shared a deep interest in art, "everything was under the sign of art. She was constantly talking about books . . . And she was interested in every single aspect of art life! Auctions, art books, new exhibitions, small galleries, going to the theater on Broadway, off-Broadway, off-off Broadway and so on."

As a book editor, Jackie wrote the introduction to *Atget's Gardens*, "Eugene Atget, the imagier, has caught that vanished past and allowed us to experience the beauty of the French garden which reaches back through a thousand years of civilization. That he did it with another French invention and art form, the photograph, only compounds our pleasure and our admiration. Of the arts of France, Edith Wharton said we had only to look around us and 'see that the whole world is full of her split glory.' Atget's gardens are part of that largesse." Alain Malraux observes, "She will remain as someone who had a big French inheritance, cultural inheritance that she was totally capable to appreciate the best France can offer. When I met Jacqueline Kennedy, she had a personal faculty to let you share her "art de vivre". It was her life, and she was ready to share it with every single person capable to share it and enjoy it. This is quite rare." Jackie's fascination with French history culminated in five volumes authored by her friend Olivier Bernier, *Louis XIV: A Royal Life, Secrets of Marie Antoinette, At the Court of Napoleon, The 18th Century Women,* and *Pleasure and Privilege.*

Andre Malraux, a World War II war hero, would have appreciated the photography journal Jackie commissioned by Antony Beever and Artemis Cooper, *Paris After the Liberation, 1944 to 1949.* Jackie, as a young traveler, toured the damage after World War II and later observed, "I was at school in Paris, and it was still very much the same city. If you live through a certain history, that time crystallizes later for you, and you want to know more about it."

Alain described his step-father Malraux, France's first Minister of Culture, "as a beloved philosopher of art and magic." It is true that his novels and volumes on art history position Malraux as France's most illustrious 'ecrivan engage'. Of the twenty-five volumes he wrote, the following were translated into English securing Malraux's reputation among 20th century French and

American literature: *The Conquerors, Man's Fate, The Royal Way, Days of Wrath, Man's Hope, The Psychology of Art, The Voices of Silence, The Metamorphosis of the Gods,* in 1961 he had completed *The Temptation of the West,* of course *The Museum Without Walls* and *Anti-memoirs* were not published until 1968.

In 1961, Jacqueline Kennedy, a French literature major, told Nicole Alphand the wife of the French Ambassador to the United States during the Kennedy years, "I am deeply impressed by *Les Conquerants* and *La Condition humaine.* I know every corner of the *Musee imaginaire.*"

Alain Malraux discussed how rarely foreigners speak and understand French very well, but Jackie was an exception: "She had this special gift to get nuances in French, and the right words. You know, she was so quick, and always with this apparent facility and way of being natural in every single moment."

The adventures of Andre Malraux before he met Jack and Jacqueline Kennedy inspire many to hail him as France's Hemingway. When he was twenty-two, he set out for the Far East with a secret plan to survey along the Royal Way the 'lost' archeological temple ruins of Bantai Frey in Cambodia near Angkor Wat. After Malraux attempted to leave the country with several keepsakes, he stood trial for thievery. Angered by French exploitation in Indochina, Malraux published a revolutionary newsletter *L'Indochine* in support of Ho Chi Minh's anti-French colonialist movement and was nearly burned alive in 1927 by Chiang Kai-shek for his underground association with the Communists. When he was barely thirty-two, he won France's highest literary award, the Prix Goncourt for *Man's Fate.* He and a pilot friend once borrowed a plane on a madcap adventure to fly over the deserts of Arabia in search of the Queen of Sheba's mythical capital. He arrived in Madrid two days after the outbreak of the Spanish Civil War to build up an arsenal of foreign airplane squadrons. To raise money, he starred in his own propaganda war 'documentary' by raking enemy fascist lines with a pistol as he leaned out of the cockpit of a plane he could barely steer. During the French Resistance in World War II, he harassed the Germans as the legendary underground leader "Colonel Berger". Barely escaping death, he was captured, detained, and tortured by the Nazis. He once told the New York *Times* columnist, C.L. Sulzberger, "It will not be a bad monument if, when I die, I have left one hundred new museums in France behind me."

Shortly after John Kennedy's inauguration, Herve Alphand, who presided over Washington D.C.'s French Embassy from 1956 to 1965, was received formally at the White House. President Kennedy expressed his wish to maintain the closest relations with France in every field. After a survey of the immediate problems, Kennedy said, "My first visit outside the American continent should be to France. I want to see General de Gaulle, whom I don't know, but I have read all his books, and his opinions will be extremely useful to me as I begin my term of office."

Jacqueline Bouvier left Paris a student at La Sorbonne, to return as First Lady of America. She consulted with Nicole Alphand stating that she particularly wished to meet Andre Malraux, "to hear the comments of the French writer she most admired on the masterpieces with which she studied herself". Her main area of study at George Washington University was French literature. Madame Alphand made her wishes known to Malraux, who at once signified his agreement.

Ten days before the President and Jackie were scheduled to depart for France, Pierre Salinger invited a French journalist M. Cremosse to interview the First Lady. Jackie, a tri-linguist, gave a tour of the White House and spoke in French about her admiration for foreign students. Pierre Salinger sent the tapes to Paris and Jackie's interview was broadcast all over France. On May 30, 1961, the White House entourage departed for Paris, the young Kennedy couple radiant with compassion, were at the head of the most powerful nation on earth 'with every heart at their command'.

The citizens of Paris planned for days to give the Americans an affectionate and triumphant welcome. Rose Fitzgerald Kennedy's arrival at Orly airport was timed to meet her son's plane. At 10:00

a.m. Air Force One appeared in the sky and Rose Kennedy, Boston's proud Fitzgerald matriarch, was well-positioned to greet her son. She watched Jack and Jackie exchange a warm welcome with General de Gaulle, when suddenly she caught her son's expression. She once confided, "I thought he looked a little surprised when he spotted me, but he gave me a big grin. Yet I expect he wasn't very surprised, even when three chairs were brought forward and I was asked to sit with Jackie and Yvonne De Gaulle while the photographers whirred away at us."

General and Yvonne de Gaulle with President and Jacqueline Kennedy rode through the streets of Paris, past the Place de la Concorde, led by a cavalry of the plumed Republican Guard. A holiday had been declared in honor of the American visit and over five hundred thousand people chanted, "Vive Jacqueline! Vive le President!"

At the Elysee Palace, on May 31st, while the President and First Lady were greeting the guests, they learned that a tragic car accident killed Malraux's two sons a few days before the Kennedy's arrival. Jacqueline discovered that the Minister was in mourning, and she offered to cancel his private museum tour for her. Then Andre and Madeleine Malraux passed by discreetly into the crowd. Malraux's astonishing courage in overcoming his grief to fulfill his duty as Minister of Culture deeply moved Jacqueline Kennedy.

The next evening, the Palace of Versailles, once a simple hunting lodge for King Louis XIV, set the stage for General and Madame de Gaulle's soiree to honor the President, Jacqueline and one hundred and fifty guests. A vision of opulence, the palace ignites tales of Louis XIV's legendary patronage of Louis Le Vau to build a spectacular monument to the French classical style of the mid-17th century with formal gardens designed by Andre Le Notre. From 1682 until 1790, the palace was the official residence of the kings of France. Jacqueline Kennedy studied the memoirs of the Duc de Saint-Simon, an aristocrat who wrote about Louis XIV's ceremonies of the royal court. He once said, "with an almanac and a watch, even at a distance of three hundred leagues, you could say precisely what the king was doing". After the American Revolutionary War of 1776, the painter Couder's allegory, *The Capture of York Town*, was installed in Versailles' Hall of Battles. George Washington, La Fayette and Rochambeau stand united after defeating the British in the decisive battle at Yorktown with the pivotal support of French military. The French aristocracy ruled at Versailles until 1789 when revolutionary mobs killed the guards, captured Louis XVI and Marie-Antoinette, who were guillotined in Paris. In 1833, King Louis-Philippe transformed Versailles into a Museum of French History.

The first lady elegantly coiffed in a white Givenchy gown embroidered with soft pastel flowers was radiant. The evening was like a dream, surrounded by her friends, both old and new. Throughout dinner, Jacqueline charmed de Gaulle as her husband's French interpreter. Louis XV's favorite ballet was performed in his sumptuous jewel-box theater. Then a glorious fireworks finale illuminated the gardens. As the Americans departed for Paris, music drifted through the trees, the French, and then the American national anthems carried the General's farewell.

"She was indeed a *success fou*." Rose Kennedy, who knew Paris, especially the fashion houses, decidedly remarked, "It has been said that success in any milieu involves a combination of the right person at the right place at the right time. Jackie was the woman, Paris was the place and Spring was the time. Jack was delighted, both with her and for her." De Gaulle announced, "She played the game very intelligently. Without mixing in politics, she gave her husband the prestige of Maecenas."

Jackie then received the long-awaited answer on June 2nd, Andre Malraux agreed to act as art historian to the former Sorbonne student. At the Musee de Jeu de Paume, he discussed Manet, Renoir and Cezanne. Below Manet's *Olympia*, he had placed Bouguereau's *Venus*, brought from Compiegne. *Venus* had received the Salon prize in the year which *Olympia* was refused, and the two pictures had never been shown side by side. At Malmaison, Josephine Bonaparte's country chateau, Mrs. Kennedy paused before a portrait of Josephine, and said to him in her gentle, subdued voice: "What a cruel fate! She must have been an extraordinary woman." "A real bitch," replied the Minister, as he recalled the stormy relations between Josephine and Napoleon. After Malmaison, Malraux, Nicole Alphand and Jacqueline lunched at La Celle St. Cloud the hideaway retreat of Louis XV's favorite mistress, Madame de Pompadour.

Mrs. Kennedy charmed Andre Malraux and General Charles de Gaulle with her knowledge of French language and culture. Before she left France, Jackie asked de Gaulle, "since we will probably never see you again, what do you think of us?" General de Gaulle answers her in French: "Les Anglais sont embettant. Russes inquietant. Americains fatiguent."

The Kennedy's traveled to meet Nikita Khrushchev in Vienna. Jackie visited the Imperial Spanish Riding School while the Soviet premier strong-headedly threatened to spread Communism throughout the world. In the summit meetings, Kennedy persuaded the senior statesman to join his efforts to develop an international Nuclear Test Ban Treaty. That evening an amused Jackie conversed with Soviet Premier Nikita Khrushchev before the *Blue Danube* ballet performance. Searching for conversation, Jackie asked about Pushinka, the outer space traveling Russian dog, cooing that she would love to have a puppy, since the mother was pregnant. Back in Washington, the Khruschev's gift of the Russian puppy became Jackie's most amusing cultural exchange story.

In 1962, President Kennedy planned a dinner at the White House to honor leaders in the American arts and to celebrate The White House cultural exchange success. He hoped Andre Malraux would agree to lend his presence to this event, and soon it was arranged for the month of May.

Nicole Alphand assisted Jacqueline Kennedy with her plans for the state dinner during a weekend in Palm Beach. Madame Alphand, a co-conspirator, knew that Jacqueline wished to transform the perception of the White House into an American Versailles, a mecca of culture and fine art. "We mustn't allow Andre Malraux to be bored," Jacqueline said, "and since he speaks English badly, we should first of all invite people who speak French." Madame Alphand sensed that Malraux could handle any situation and what mattered was to gather round her table the greatest artists in America, French speaking or not.

In April, during discussions in Paris with Herve Alphand, the Minister found it a fascinating prospect. Not only would he speak about culture, he would counsel President Kennedy about French politics. It was at a time when American-French opinions differed over France's plans for nuclear armaments.

The General was not prepared, in the immediate future, to return the visit which Kennedy had paid him the previous year, "but", added Malraux, "he is quite glad to send on his tanks, in other words myself, to have them set on fire to light his path."

General de Gaulle warned Kennedy in their 1961 Paris meetings that France would not be a part of any military action in Laos. In 1954 after securing military aid from both Truman and Eisenhower, French forces fighting Vietnamese rebels led by nationalist leader Ho Chi Minh were defeated. After eight years of fighting an estimated 400,000 men had died in battle. In the Geneva Accords, Laos and Cambodia were given their independence but Vietnam was divided into half with the Communists taking the North. General de Gaulle warned against what he saw as a dangerously misguided involvement in Southeast Asia. The General advised, "For you, intervention in this region will be an entanglement without end . . . I predict to you that you will, step by step, become sucked into a bottomless military and political quagmire, despite the losses and expenditures you may squander."

Before Malraux left for America, newstories swirled in Washington, New York and Paris about the new Minister of Culture's master plan. One was that the Minister dreamed of creating a galaxy of cultural centers in provincial cities with the idea of "decentralizing" French culture, just as the country's economy was being decentralized. The New York *Times* magazine speculated on the role of the first Minister of Cultural Affairs in an article dated May 6, 1962: "Until three years ago, it was the Ministry of Education that had been entrusted with the jewels in the French cultural crown as the Comedie Francaise, L'Opera, Jean Vilar's Theatre National Populaire, the National Conservatory, the Beaux Arts and the Louvre . . . the rulers of France were willing to permit the Rockefeller family, on the other side of the Atlantic, to contribute money to the badly needed restoration of Versailles and Fontainebleau . . . because the budget to restore historic monuments was the same three years ago as it was in 1908 . . . this was both humiliating and a hypocritical policy for a country which made some claim to being a cradle of the arts . . . de Gaulle in 1958 . . . named his friend and faithful follower to head it . . . they have cheered each new exhibition Malraux has promoted . . . exotic arts of the Chad . . . the Braque show . . . they cheered when he recently pried away Veronese's huge canvas from the Venetian Room in the Louvre to restore it to the salon in Versailles which Louis XIV had specially designed . . . for giving Le Corbuisier a contract to build a twenty-seven story skyscraper, . . . age-blackened stones of the Louvre lovingly restored . . . to a miraculously tender prim-rose hue. . . ."

Yet, along the way, Malraux's temperament angered the entrenched cultural monopolies in Paris. He once observed of himself: "I have always felt more at home in a revolution than a salon."

When Malraux arrived in Washington, he visited the Institute of Contemporary Arts, attended a 'stag' luncheon at the Overseas Writers Club, privately met with the director of the United States Information Agency, William R. Murrow, and was honored with a reception at the State Department. President Kennedy welcomed Andre Malraux to America as if he was a visiting head of state.

Jacqueline Kennedy wished to reciprocate Malraux's museum tour she enjoyed on her journey to Paris a year earlier. Mrs. Kennedy greeted Andre Malraux and his wife Madeleine and they joined John Walker the director of The National Gallery of Art. The gallery director wished to impress the French Minister by exhibiting, for the first time, a painting by John Copley representing the artist's family. After Malraux briefly looked at the painting, he leaned towards Jacqueline and said to her;

"Certain paintings belong to the history of humanity, others to the history of the United States. I am very happy to see this one for the *second* reason."

The National Gallery tour included Domenico Veneziano's fifteenth-century *Madonna With Child*, El Greco's *Christ Chasing the Moneylenders from the Temple* and Rembrandt's *Girl With a Broom*. As they were leaving the museum, Jackie gushed, "My favorite paintings are those *he* (Malraux) likes best."

"There was a very famous marvelous chamber music concert given by the President and Mrs. Kennedy in the White House with Isaac Stern." Alain Malraux observes, "After that, my parents had been very impressed by the natural elegance and the way Mrs. Kennedy got involved in the arts, and it was a new way to add something to public life which came from Mrs. Kennedy."

Luminaries in the arts and sciences gathered on the evening of May 11, 1962 at the White House to honor Andre Malraux. Arthur Miller, Andrew Wyeth, Tennessee Williams, Thornton Wilder, Paddy Chayefsky, Stephane Boudin, Saul Bellow, Elia Kazan, Robert Lowell, Andre Meyer, Robert Lehman, George Balanchine, Raymond Bonham-Carter, Lee Strasberg, Miss Susan Strasberg and Geraldine Page were among the guests. Isaac Stern borrowed a fiddle from the Air Force Strolling Strings to play an impromptu recital. He then joined Leonard Rose and Eugene Istomin to perform Franz Schubert's Trio in B Flat major, Opus 99 for violin, cello and piano.

Madame Malraux was seated on the right of President Kennedy in the State Dining Room. In the Blue Room, Andre Malraux was on Jacqueline Kennedy's right. Much to Minister Malraux's confused amusement, President Kennedy's toast could not be heard in the Blue Room: " I want to tell you how very pleased we are to have so many distinguished writers and artists and actresses and creative thinkers. You know, one of the great myths of American life is that nothing is easier than lying around all day and painting a picture or writing a book and leading a rather easy life. In my opinion the ultimate in self-discipline is a creative work. There are so many more people playing instruments now, going to symphonies,

going to the theater, to art galleries, painting, than anyone real-
izes. And it is our hope that Americans will begin to look about
them and realize that here in these years we are building a life
which, as I say, develops the maximum in each individual."

President Kennedy pays homage to Malraux, "Now we have
the best model that we could have this evening in welcoming
Monsieur and Madame Malraux." Jack Kennedy admired
Malraux for his unusual adventures in life, and observes that,
"We are the descendants of early founders who were themselves
men of great variety and vitality. But Monsieur Malraux has
led an archeological expedition to Cambodia, been connected
with Chiang Kai-shek, Mao Tse-tung, and has been active in
the Spanish Civil War, participated in the defense of his country during World War II when the Germans invaded France,
now he is a trusted advisor to General de Gaulle, and has been
at the same time a great creative figure in his own right. He has
left, I think, most of us way behind."

In response to Kennedy's warm toast Andre Malraux remarked: "I thank you for having welcomed me here by your
masterpieces and, better yet, by your masterpieces as presented
by Mrs. Kennedy. I have been received here as I have never
been before.".

Malraux, the philosopher-historian, gives his impression of
America: "The United States is the country that assumes the des-
tiny of man." From the author who wrote the celebrated novel,
Man's Fate, this was an extraordinary compliment. "Through the
millennia many countries have achieved first place by sustained
efforts, at the price of innumerable human lives. There has been an
Assyrian Empire, a Byzantine Empire, a Roman Empire. There is
no American Empire. There is, however, the United States. For the
first time a country has become the world's leader without achiev-
ing this through conquest. And it is strange to think that for thousands of years one single country has found power while seeking
only justice . . ."

Malraux's 1962 journey was an inspiration for Jackie, who hoped to model her expansion of culture on Malraux's programs in Paris with federal and state funding. This was Malraux's hope as well. The Kennedy's invited Andre and Madeleine Malraux to spend Sunday with them privately at their country home Glen Ora in Virginia. Malraux was able to explain the French position to the President as this had emerged from his discussions with General de Gaulle in Paris in '61. They touched on a wide range of subjects: Europe and the West, the Soviet Union, India and China. The general's idea was that France needed nuclear independence to reinforce her international position. De Gaulle wanted "to give back to France its voice as a great power by adapting it to the world of today, and preparing it for the world of tomorrow."

Before Malraux left, the press invited the Minister to answer a great number of questions, all of them political except one. This was the last:

"And if we expressed the wish to see Leonardo da Vinci's *Mona Lisa* in the United States, what would you say?"

"Yes, without hesitation," replied Andre Malraux. Either it would be technically impossible, he thought, and this would be easy to prove, or it would be possible, and everyone would be thrilled. In any case the General would certainly relish the idea. So the rendezvous was set, and the promise was kept.

Andre Malraux personally devoted extraordinary care to organizing the journey of the most famous painting in the world. Italian genius, Leonardo da Vinci's, *Mona Lisa* traveled like a sovereign. Experts were dispatched before her arrival to examine with John Walker, the director of The National Gallery of Art, the conditions of her transport and custody. Never for a moment did her guardians lose sight of the thermometer and hygrometer. The Italian mason who had kidnapped her at the beginning of the century, and hidden her for several months under his bed in a house in the north of Italy, had not taken so many precautions—and still she had survived. But the instructions of the Ministry were "nothing must be left to chance".

Alain Malraux joined his parents to greet the *Mona Lisa* in America, he remembers, "In 1963, Jackie Kennedy, the President, and the Malraux's were reunited for the third occasion to show America the *Mona Lisa*. It was a very official gesture for Andre Malraux to send the most famous painting in the world by Leonardo da Vinci. It was his way to underline the links between the two countries. Malraux was extremely, something not so French I would say, he was extremely grateful for the American contribution and a decisive one in World War II and before."

On January 9, 1963, the day of the private viewing at The National Gallery of Art, Andre Malraux gave a poignant speech: "If, upon my return, I am asked before the Assembly by some peevish deputy, 'Why risk lending the *Mona Lisa* to the United States?'"

Malraux confides to his audience, "There were greater risks involved by the American boys who landed at Arromanches—without mentioning those who preceded them in World War I—these risks were much more certain. To the humblest among them, who may be listening tonight, I want to say, without lifting my voice, that the masterpiece to which, Mr. President, you are paying a historic tribute this evening is a painting your soldiers have saved."

Malraux speaks to the heroes of our past, "It is the soldier who saved the painting we pay homage to tonight."

President Kennedy responded to Malraux's words: "France and America have been on the same side for four wars and we believe in the same democratic credos. At the time of the painting, Columbus was discovering the New World. This painting before us spans the whole life of the New World. We, the unknown nation at the time of its creation, are its inheritors and its protectors of the ideals which gave it birth. Its creator embodied in it, the central purpose of our civilization . . . to preserve the chief gift of nature which is liberty. And in this belief, Leonardo da Vinci expressed the profound belief of our two nations. It is shown that the worlds of art and politics are one. Malraux comes as an emissary from General de Gaulle who has taken his position among the few Western statesman who grasp the meaning and possibility of the past, and thus are able to shape the course of our society . . ."

Over the next few days, more than a million visitors filed past the *Mona Lisa* and Andre Malraux's daring decision to let her cross the Atlantic was fully rewarded. Alain Malraux had a unique chance to meet the Kennedy's: "When I went to see the *Mona Lisa*, always thanks to the banker Andre Meyer, there was a private dinner. I was allowed to go and that was my first souvenir of Mrs. Kennedy. Andre Malraux, my mother, me and Andre Meyer went to a most charming dinner party. One could see by listening to Jackie Kennedy how important art had been since she was a young girl in her twenties. How much she considered art as a very essential part of her life before President Kennedy was elected, during his presidency and I know that after his assassination, too."

The Malraux's continued to New York City with the *Mona Lisa*. The Metropolitan Museum of Art was to play host to the Italian Lady. In New York, on Tuesday, May 15, to commemorate the 50th anniversary of the Alliance Francaise (French Institute), Malraux gave a long speech about the 'American dream', the role of the artist and the effects of popularizing culture.

Andre Malraux, Madeleine and Alain returned to Paris and eleven months later President Kennedy was assassinated. "Malraux and my mother have been, like everyone else, extremely impressed by the way she attended to this funeral. It was not enough to say it was moving. It's striking when you think of her thirty years after. Let's face it, she is very brave. And she was always going, how can I say it in English? She was always going "de l'avant", moving ahead."

Alain Malraux recalls his parents' memories of Jacqueline Kennedy: "Malraux could not speak about personal tragedies. He had so many tragedies in his life. He was impressed by the way she proved herself to be calm and to overcome things, events, situations. But, I think they would share practical jokes or they would speak on big subjects, but not personal ones. They had a sort of wit. Like great actors, it's in the way they play the text."

In 1967, Andre Malraux, the progenitor of France's cultural rebirth, dedicated his American edition of *Anti-memoirs* to Mrs. Jacqueline Kennedy. Alain Malraux observes, "He had given a certain importance to the English edition of his *Anti-memoirs*. There was a personal purpose. It was to show the whole world that he was her friend and admirer."

A SHARED LOVE FOR ARTISTS & WRITERS

Jacqueline Bouvier loved writers so much she aspired to be a journalist and then she married one. After her first year of being married, her anniversary gift to her husband was a leather bound collection of his early Senate speeches. She wrote a poem that ended, "for he must go seeking the Golden Fleece." As a couple they admired each other's literary interests, reading Winston Churchill, Charles de Gaulle, Talleyrand and many other historians, literary figures, and sharing passages of verse from Edith Hamilton's *The Greek Way*.

Jackie's taste in literature and world history were shaped and inspired while she attended Vassar College. Her two favorite courses were History of Religion and Lectures on Shakespeare. At one time, she memorized all the great passages in *Antony and Cleopatra* and quoted Shakespeare while observing of her husband, "His delights were dolphin-like. He showed his back above the element he lived in."

"BRING HIM BACK-IT'S YOUR LAST CHANCE"

The 1947 summer after her freshman year at Vassar, Jackie made her first Grand Tour of Europe. In London, Jackie and her traveling party were invited to a Royal Garden Party at Buckingham Palace to presumably be 'presented' to King George IV and Queen Elizabeth. But the crowds and the rain made it impossible, so the young girls slowly marched through the receiving line, smiling as they passed the Queen. When Jackie spotted Winston Churchill in the receiving line, she quickly returned to the end of the line, stopping to get her chance to shake his hand. The party continued to tour Paris, then the chateau country, and upon arrival at the French Riviera, Winston Churchill appeared again when they visited Juan-les-Pins.

She soon returned to France in 1949 as an exchange student to attend summer classes at the University de Grenoble, continuing her studies in Paris at La Sorbonne. The most distinguished college within The University of Paris, the college specializes in teaching French civilization and French literature, and its professors are considered 'world famous'. Robert de Sorbonne, the private chaplain to Louis IX, founded the theology school in 1250. Jean Paul Sartre and Simone de Beauvoir's existentialism, a new philosophy of 'existence over essence' permeated every old street in Paris, calling for people to be judged by their actions, not their words. By 1949 Andre Malraux was a legendary World War II war hero and author.

Jacqueline once said, "It was the best year of my life." She chose to live with a French family, where only the native language was spoken. She found a loving family in the home of Comtesse de Renty, and discovered a lasting friendship with the Comtesse's daughter Claude. In 1951, Jackie acted as tour guide for her sister Lee, and they memorialized their summer trip to Europe in a journal *One Special Summer*. After Lee and Jackie visited the art historian Bernard Berenson near Florence, Jackie remarked, "The two most impressive people I have ever met are Bernard Berenson and Charles de Gaulle."

Jacqueline Bouvier left Vassar to attend George Washington University. Janet Auchincloss suggested she enter *Vogue* magazine's Prix de Paris writing contest. Jackie was one of four first prize winners. The editors were intrigued by her choice of people she admired; Diaghilev, Oscar Wilde and Charles Baudelaire, a Russian ballet impresario who escaped to Paris after the fall of the Romanov dynasty, an exiled homosexual Irish playwright, and a French poet. Jack Kennedy's first serious attempt at writing began during the early conflicts precipitating World War II. His father, Joseph P. Kennedy, was appointed by President Franklin Roosevelt as the first Irish Catholic Ambassador to the Court of St. James. When war broke out in Europe, Jack, intrigued by the clash of London politics over Germany, deferred his junior year at Harvard to observe the political scene first-hand in London. He returned to Harvard to write his senior honors thesis in government and chose to describe the British history precipitating the lack of political vision causing the failure of the Munich Pact and World War II. The thesis was expanded into a book titled *Why England Slept* that became a best-seller.

Ambassador Kennedy's isolationist position towards Germany reflected the British government's attitude of pacifism after the economic recovery from World War I. In his analysis Jack Kennedy pointed out the weak leadership of British Prime Minister Stanley Baldwin, and then Chamberlain's illusion of a guaranteed peace in the Munich Pact. Kennedy wrote: "The situation came to a head in March when Hitler invaded Prague. It now became evident to all that the hope of a permanent peace for Europe was doomed. The invasion of Prague meant the end of the Chamberlain policy of appeasement . . . and England was determined to resist German attempts at Expansion. " The young Kennedy praised Winston Churchill for challenging the status quo. He analyzed the control of a totalitarian government vs. a democracy, the pacifist attitude of the British people, and the policy of disarmament vs. rearmament. Kennedy concludes that unpreparedness compounded by public apathy during an economic boom in England were the chief causes. A pacifist outlook, bolstered by the losses sustained during World War I, Kennedy argues, swayed the English into a perilous position in regards to the Nazi menace.

After college, in 1952, Jackie found her early writing ambitions rewarded at the Washington *Times-Herald* as the Inquiring Camera Girl. She reported to the editor of the paper Frank Waldrop, who once hired Kathleen Kennedy, Jack's younger sister. One day, Waldrop assigned her to go to Congress to interview Vice President Nixon and newly elected Senator Jack Kennedy. Her satirical wit was in good company, when she asked two pages, "What's it like to observe the Senators at close range?" Jerry Hoobler said of Kennedy, "He's always being taken for a tourist because he looks so young. The other day he wanted to use the special phones, but the guards told him, 'Sorry mister these are reserved for Senators.'"

John Kennedy's second book, a biography of his brother Joe's life, *As We Remember Him,* tells the story of his death during World War II as a Patrol Plane Commander and expert in radio control projects: "at the time of his death, Joe had completed probably more combat missions in heavy bombers than any other pilot in his rank in the Navy and therefore was preeminently qualified . . ." The book demonstrates the family's ambition to move beyond the accumulation of wealth to the highest level of public service was engineered by the father Joseph P. Kennedy. Rose Fitzgerald Kennedy's long-standing involvement with Boston politics may have been the true genesis of the Kennedy family ambition. Her father John Francis Fitzgerald nicknamed, Honey Fitz, was the first Irish Catholic mayor of Boston. Professor Harold Laski of the London School of Economics is quoted in the book: "Joe often sat in my study and submitted, with that smile that was pure magic, to relentless teasing about his determination to be nothing less than President of the United States."

Jack and Jackie shared an appreciation for poetry, and one of Alan Seeger's poems, "I have a Rendez-vous With Death," was a favorite. Jackie offers the explanation that, "the poignancy of men dying young always moved my husband . . . possibly because of Joe . . . he did not know when his own rendez-vous with death might come." After Jack survived childhood illnesses, then barely recuperating from his World War II injuries, Joe Kennedy once said about his son, "I've stood by his deathbed four times. Each time I've said goodbye to him, he always came back."

By 1957, the American public appetite for Kennedy family 'news' reached a state of fascination that would keep gossip columnists and social historians busy for years to come. One article, 'Rules for Visiting the Kennedys' captures the public's intrigue: "Prepare yourself by reading the *Congressional Record, U.S. News and World Report, Time, Newsweek, Fortune, The Nation,* 'How To Play Sneaky Tennis' and The Democratic Digest, then memorize at least six good jokes, anticipate that you may be required to advise one of the Kennedy's on their a) hair-do, b) dress, c) backhand and d) latest public achievement. Be sure to answer, 'Terrific'."

Jackie enrolled in American history and political science studies at Georgetown University to broaden her knowledge, and to better understand research projects her husband wanted her to handle. Then, in 1956, Senator Kennedy suffered a long and debilitating illness after a spinal operation that required months of bedrest for a complete recovery. His health was so severely weakened that a priest was summoned to give him his last rites, but providence intervened. During this period of immobility, he read a biography of Kansas Senator Edmund Ross, who committed political suicide by casting the single vote that prevented the impeachment of President Andrew Johnson. Senator Ross' explanation for his action as a way to protect, "the highest good of the country," impressed the young Senator so much that he decided to write a history of eight Senators who demonstrated professional courage. Kennedy adopted Hemingway's idea of courage "grace under pressure." The eight senators profiled include: John Quincy Adams, Daniel Webster, Thomas Hart Benton, Sam Houston, Edmund G. Ross,

Lucius Quintus Cincinnatus Lamar, George Norris and Robert A. Taft. The concept of *Profiles In Courage* was to chronicle unpopular positions held against a powerful opposing majority and the sacrifice of careerism to adhere to a principal that protects the Constitution.

Jackie conducted independent research and read extensive background information from The Library of Congress to her husband. Dave Powers recalled, "She'd sit down at his bedside and read to him for hours from the material that was to become the book." *Profiles In Courage* was awarded a Pulitzer Prize elevating John F. Kennedy into national prestige as a man of letters. The five hundred dollar prize money was donated to the United Negro College Fund. The history book is one of the all-time best-sellers totaling over five million copies in 1965. Among those he thanked, Arthur Krock, Arthur Schlesinger, Professor James McGregor Burns, the greatest debt to Theodore Sorensen, and his wife Jacqueline Kennedy. He states, "This book would not have been possible without the encouragement, assistance and criticism offered from the very beginning by my wife, whose help during all the days of my convalescence I cannot ever adequately acknowledge." After the success of *Profiles In Courage,* the junior Senator was chosen to give Adlai Stevenson's nomination speech at the next Democratic Convention in 1956, and nearly chosen as Vice President.

On his losing the vice presidential nomination, Jack's philosophical nature prevailed: "Joe, Jr. was the star of our family. He did everything better than the rest of us. If he had lived he would have gone on in politics and he would have been elected to the house and senate as I was. And, like me, he would have gone for the vice-presidential nomination at the 1956 convention. But unlike me, he wouldn't have been beaten . . . Joe would have won . . ."

In the Spring of 1958, Jack and Jackie were invited to a cocktail party to honor Winston Churchill on the *Christina*, Aristotle Onassis yacht, docked at Skorpios. Onassis was impressed with Jackie, later remarking, "There's something provocative about that lady, she's got a carnal soul." Churchill ignored Jack Kennedy at the party. That did not deter the young Senator, "Winston Churchill is one of my husband's heroes," Jackie later confided to her biographer Mary Van Rensselaer Thayer in 1960. "He admires Sir Winston as a man of letters and has read every written Churchillian word."

"You be Kennedy and I'll be Spivak," Senator Kennedy told a guest before he was to appear on Lawrence Spivak's television program, "Meet The Press". Kennedy continued acting as Spivak, "All right Horatio Alger, just what makes you think you want to be President?" John F. Kennedy's most powerful ally was often his own wit, intelligence, and, central to his personality, a strong self-knowledge gained from his life's journey .

In 1959, Kennedy warned America about the Russian's innovative cultural exchange programs. He describes how the United States failed to cultivate a prestigious international identity: "The cultural program is part of this. They have spent more than one half billion dollars over the past few years to send their artists, dancers, and other performers all over the world. We have allotted two to three million a year for this purpose. Russia spent fifty million on their exhibition at the Brussels World's Fair, the United States spent fourteen million."

Eleanor Roosevelt wrote in her autobiography, *My Days*: "We need emotional outlets in this country, and the more artistic people we develop, the better it will be for us as a nation." Franklin Delano Roosevelt's successful Works Progress Administration program inspired the Kennedy's plans for a national policy to expand cultural exchange and federal funding of the arts.

In 1960, during his hectic election campaign, that John F. Kennedy found time to write, edit and review a compilation of his Senate speeches on foreign affairs is a testament to his formidable determination, the depth of his convictions and the loyalty of his staff. *The Strategy of Peace* edited by Columbia University historian Allen Nivens, who once aided Adlai Stevenson, was hailed by a former Republican pro-Humphrey professor: "*The Strategy of Peace* is incontestably the best campaign document I can imagine, for it communicates what various other books and most news reports inadequately convey . . . Kennedy emerges from that book as the kind of reflective and purposeful candidate that many of us seek." The Senator employed Jackie as she said to translate, "the speech on Indochina, because so much of the source material was in French. I did the same for his Algerian speech." A mass mailing in the Spring of 1960 included editors, scientists, columnists, educators, reporters, authors, publishers, labor leaders, clergymen, and public opinions leaders.

In 1959, Leonard Bernstein's New York Philharmonic orchestra performed eighteen concerts in the USSR. In 1960, Russian born Isaac Stern began his long crusade to save Carnegie Hall. In 1961, ballet virtuoso Rudolph Nureyev defected from Russia. In 1962, American Ballet Theater journeyed as the first ballet company to tour Russia. That same year Leonard Bernstein, with the First Lady in attendance, celebrated the opening of Avery Fisher Hall in the Lincoln Center for Performing Arts complex. Both Jackie and Jack Kennedy recognized that artists could be employed to do the work of missionaries by soothing hostile countries feelings with American cultural exchange programs.

The Kennedy's cultivated writers and artists presuming both professions shared common goals: to enlighten and to foster a deeper understanding of the human condition and guide public opinion to alleviate the problems in a society whether it be racism, poverty, chauvinism or apathy. The Kennedy White House was deeply connected to the creative world. He labored over his speeches, wrote books and articles to document and clarify his ideas, and he courted the best writers of fiction and non-fiction as his supporters. His joy in reading Ian Flemings' famous British spy novels about James Bond's adventures is legendary, but Norman Mailer was pleasantly surprised at the Democratic Convention in 1960 when

Kennedy spoke to him about *Deer Park*. Kennedy also discussed with James Michener *The Fires of Spring* and Eugene Burdick about *The Ninth Wave*. Yet, Theodore Sorensen reports that among his favorites were *Talleyrand, Marlborough* and *Melbourne* and he studied *The Guns of August* an account of the origins of World War I.

Jacqueline Kennedy cared deeply about poetry and literature. Her interest in eighteenth century history and French politics was heightened while attending the Sorbonne. A lifelong Francophile, she read extensively with an emphasis on French manners, culture, politics and art during her entire life. When Jackie and President Kennedy invited the forty-nine living Nobel Peace prize winners to the White House, Diana Trilling recalled that Jackie cornered her husband to discuss his favorite writers. She proceeded to privately grilled the Columbia professor, Lionel Trilling about which of D.H. Lawrence's novels was his favorite, specifically asking about *Lady Chatterly's Lover*. Professor Trilling sent Jackie a copy of D. H. Lawrence's *The Rainbow*, and then in 1965 she received his essays, *Beyond Culture: Essays on Literature and Learning*.

Mary Hemingway, an honored guest at the April 1962 Nobel dinner, permitted Fredric March to read the opening of her husband's unpublished work "Islands in the Stream". Additional readings of Nobel winners included Sinclair Lewis and George C. Marshall. "Few Americans have had greater impact on the emotions and attitudes of the American people than Ernest Hemingway . . ." President Kennedy's posthumous tribute recaptured that Hemingway's definition of courage 'grace under pressure' had once inspired Kennedy's writing. On October 28, 1954 Hemingway was awarded the Nobel Prize for Literature. He was too ill to receive the award in Stockholm but held a party at Finca Vigia, his home in Cuba. After Hemingway left Cuba in July 1960, his mental health succumbed to a long struggle with depression and alcohol. On November 30th, 1960, Ernest Hemingway was treated at the Mayo Clinic with electric shock therapy. After the proscribed cure, he lost his memory, and discovered he could no longer function as a writer. Kennedy had invited Hemingway to the Presidential Inauguration in 1960 but the author was too ill to attend. Hemingway killed himself in a log cabin in Ketcham, Idaho on Sunday July 2nd,1961.

Among President and Mrs. Kennedy's dinner guests on April 29, 1962 were Pearl Buck, Robert Frost, Mrs. George C. Marshall, Nobel Peace Prize winner Lester Pearson of Canada, Dr. Robert Oppenheimer, Astronaut Lt. Col. John H. Glenn, Jr., Dr. Linus Pauling, William Styron, James Baldwin, John Dos Passos, Norman Cousins, Katherine Anne Porter, Lionel and Diana Trilling, Ralph Bunche, and Samuel Eliot Morison. Pearl Buck author of *The Good Earth* was the first American woman to receive the Nobel Prize for Literature in 1938. The stellar array of guests inspired President Kennedy's remark that it was "the most extraordinary collection of talent, of human knowledge, that has ever gathered at the White House, with the possible exception of when Thomas Jefferson dined alone."

Nobel winner, Linus Pauling, in hopes of advancing an end to the atmospheric testing of nuclear weapons, picketed the White House on the day of the Nobel dinner. Pauling expressed his peace activism in a petition delivered to the United Nations in 1957. He had collected the signatures of 11,021 scientists from all over the world. His campaign led to a second Nobel Peace Prize in 1962, inspiring the first Nuclear Test Ban Treaty. The controversy over Pauling's activity on the day of the dinner stirred the curiosity of the president's daughter Caroline. Jackie reported the little girl was wondering: "What has Daddy done now?"

The President's five year old daughter was a very good reader. Both mother and daughter especially appreciated the French author and illustrator Ludwig Bemelsman who created the famous orphan Madeline. The verse is instructive, "They smiled at the good and frowned at the bad, and sometimes they were very sad. They left the house at half-past nine, in two straight lines, in rain or shine . . . The smallest one was Madeline." Caroline's memory was so retentive that her father taught her the lines of a poem by Edna St. Vincent Millay: "Safe upon the solid rock the ugly houses stand, Come and see my shining palace built upon the sand," and he promised to include it in one of his speeches.

Le « Whashington Post » avait groupé dans ce dessin satirique les plus célèbres invités d'Onassis. Au premier rang, Jackie et John Kennedy, Margaret et Tony, le prince Rainier et la princesse Grace, Greta Garbo, Churchill. Au second rang, Lee Radziwill, Cary Grant, Margot Fonteyn, Onassis lui-même et Maria Callas, Richard Burton et Liz Taylor.

In American history, John F. Kennedy's books remain the best-selling of any president with Ulysses S. Grant a distant second. Woodrow Wilson, one of Kennedy's heroes, wrote at age twenty-eight his impressive *Congressional Government.* President Wilson distinguished himself as an astute political analyst beyond John F. Kennedy's ability, and in that area of expertise James Madison and Thomas Jefferson are in a league all their own. But then, so is Kennedy, because he was more interested in popularizing historical biography and never considered himself a profound social philosopher. His desired effect was to educate broad areas of complex political thought and his style is more direct like Teddy Roosevelt and Harry Truman. He was not a ivory tower philosopher, but a thinker of what action to take to achieve a specific desired result. In the tradition of Winston Churchill, Kennedy was consumed with forecasting the impact of a nation's specific actions.

While she was first lady, Jackie commissioned *The White House: An Historic Guide.* The first history of McKim, Mead and White's Beaux Arts designed White House was conceived and published under the editorial guidance of Jacqueline Kennedy to offset the costs of renovating and restoring the nation's most famous mansion. The guide is in its 19th edition and has sold over 4,400,000 copies to date, it is her first best-selling book. The earnings from its publication has provided funds for important paintings and furnishings for the White House since its publication.

While Jackie was in the White House, her most comprehensive contribution was setting forth a civic plan for the preservation of the nation's capital. Arthur Schlesinger, Jr. notes that, "Jackie saw the White House itself not as a private residence, but as a possession of the American people, and she renewed its historical continuities." Her efforts to expand the jurisdiction of the Department of the Interior, headed by Stewart Udall, are described in the following documents: *Program for the Historic Preservation of Lafayette Square including Design of Federal Office Building, The White House Collection: Preliminary Catalog, Furniture, Furnishings, Fine Arts Acquired 1961 to Nov. 1964* and *The White House Library: A Short Title List.*

Kennedy's advisor on Latin America, Arthur Schlesinger, Jr., acted as one of the scholars to compile a list of books for the Presidential Library most essential to understand America's national literary past. *The White House Library: A Short Title List* is not a list of delicate antique editions, but recently published American literature selected to create a working library. Both President Kennedy and Jackie chose not to maintain a rare book collection, so that the library books could circulate, and the momentum would be to collect modern American authors as well as those from the past.

Program for the Historic Preservation of Lafayette Square including Design of Federal Office Building sets forth Jackie Kennedy's first design project supervised by the architect John Carl Warneke to preserve the homes and the buildings surrounding Lafayette Square, the Old Executive Office Building and the court house which is now the Renwick Galley. Her restoration plans for the White House and Pennsylvania Avenue shaped the spirit of the historic heart of the nation's capital during a time when modern architects and developers mounted campaigns to demolish Washington's architectural treasures. The concept of historic preservation was gathering momentum in America, but in New York City that did not prevent Pennsylvania Station's demolition in August of 1963.

On June 8, 1962, Jacqueline Kennedy wrote a passionate twelve page letter to an old family friend, the painter William Walton. The specific purpose was to urge him to take on an active role of leadership on the Commission of Fine Arts, the federal agency authorized to review architectural and design plans for buildings and landscapes at locations of specific interest to the United States government. The letter testifies to Jackie Kennedy's deep personal commitment to preserving the beauty and history of Washington D.C.: "I don't blame you for not wanting to be head. But if you aren't head, then you are useless, as people only listen to the head . . . all the things we care about, and when Jack is gone, he won't be able to help you, and lovely buildings will be torn down, and cheesy skyscrapers will go up. Perhaps saving old buildings and having the new ones isn't the most important thing in the world—if you are waiting for the *bomb*—but I think we are always going to be waiting for the bomb and it won't ever come, so to save the old buildings, and to make the new beautiful, is terribly important."

The Fine Arts Committee for the White House included Jackie's lifelong friends, Mrs. Charles Englehard, Rachel 'Bunny' Mellon, and Mrs. Jayne B. Wrightsman. The Fine Arts Advisory Committee included national museum curators and scholars in American fine arts and antiques who advised the other committees on the provenance, history, and academic legitimacy of the objects to be donated. Two experts in the presidential collections for The Adams Papers and The Jefferson Papers advised the Fine Arts Advisory Committee. The Paintings Committee included women who admired Jackie for her missionary style devotion to pressure, coax, and charm wealthy art collectors to donate the finest paintings to The White House. One of Jackie's most valuable gifts came from Walter Annenberg, who reluctantly donated David Martin's 1767 portrait of *Benjamin Franklin* which he had recently paid $200,000. Henry Francis du Pont, who possessed a vast wealth, was the genius Curator of his private home turned into the museum, *Winterthur*. He became the most influential spokesperson for Jackie's national plea to acquire the best antiques and decorative objects that once belonged to the White House. Du Pont gave her program a deep sense of integrity as she could gracefully point to *Winterthur* as her model for The White House.

Life magazine's Hugh Sidney reported Jackie's official statement for her mission: "Everything in the White House must have a reason for being there. It would be a sacrilege merely to redecorate it—a word I hate. It must be restored, and that has nothing to do with decoration. That is a question of scholarship."

The question of French interior designer, Stephane Boudin's activities aroused the eternal question, what does a Frenchman know about American architectural restoration? In 1964, Jackie advised Lady Bird Johnson: "Maison/Jansen is the one to do it with . . . everyone else is too decoratorish . . . they are the only firm with a library of historical documents and artisans trained to execute them." The idea was that design and craftsmanship had not penetrated the American scene. While Boudin, a partner with the French interior design firm Maison/Jansen, was a true architect of restoration. His aesthetic was far more developed as an interior designer than anyone in America at that time. Of course the friction between Henry Francis du Pont and Boudin is best summed up in Du Pont's remark, "I shudder to think what Mr. Boudin would do with American furniture."

On February 14th, 1962 Jackie's CBS tour of the White House left eighty million Americans spellbound. Jackie was applauded, and the program set a new standard for live television. Although Norman Mailer cryptically wrote that "Mrs. Kennedy was badly used," Jackie never felt this way, and most people thought 1600 Pennsylvania Avenue was the center-piece of the Kennedy administration cultural renaissance. *The White House Collection: Preliminary Catalog, Furniture, Furnishings, Fine Arts Acquired 1961 to Nov. 1964* documents Jackie's distinguished scholarship in her preservation of the White House.

"I never dreamed anything so perfect could happen," wrote Jacqueline Kennedy to John Loeb who funded the restoration of the Yellow Oval Room. President Kennedy referred to it as his 'easy room' and although it was located in the private living quarters, he often conducted his formal meetings there. The style of the interior was designed to model a French Louis XVI drawing room, blending an air of regal elegance with a soft color scheme. The Kennedy's often entertained especially admired guests upstairs in the Oval Room after state dinners. After the Nobel dinner, guests including Diana and Lionel Trilling were invited to Jackie's treasured Louis XVI salon. Diana Trilling once recalled that her salon upstairs was, "Jackie's chance to have a little fun."

President Kennedy published *To Turn the Tide*, a compilation of his speeches from his election through the 1961 adjournment of Congress, setting forth the goals of his first legislative year.

Jackie's favorite speeches included the inaugural address and the
American University speech on the Nuclear Test Ban Treaty,
Kennedy referred to it as his 'peace speech'. The poet Carl Sandberg
wrote the foreward and Kennedy discusses his primary concerns
in foreign affairs and his efforts to diffuse the Cold War. Carl
Sandberg observes that: "Kennedy's speeches rank in content, sub-
stance and style with those of Jefferson, Lincoln, Wilson and both
FDR and Theodore Roosevelt . . . and the President's words on
foreign policy are certainly to be heard and acted upon by more
than one audience . . ."

In 1962, the United States Information Agency distributed a
comic strip book biography of President Kennedy. The idea was to
personify Kennedy as 'Superman' with the effect of inspiring children and adults to take physical fitness more seriously. An amusing idea, the results of this 'biography' have yet to be studied.

During the presidency, the book *Creative America* edited by
Jackie and Jack's friend LeMoyne Billings, documents the plans
for a National Culture Center. The original plan for the performing arts center was conceived during the Eisenhower administration and Jacqueline Kennedy was a fervent supporter of the goal
to pass a bill to fund its construction. The article written by John
F. Kennedy "The Arts In America", and essays by James Baldwin
and Robert Frost set down the principles that inspired a national
performing arts center to be built on the Potomac River. In 1962,
overwhelming public support set in motion preliminary legisla-
ture for a Presidential Advisory Committee on the Arts which
later became the National Endowment for the Arts and Humanities during President Johnson's administration. After the assassination of President Kennedy the National Culture Center was
named as his memorial and The John F. Kennedy Center for the
Performing Arts was built during the Johnson, Nixon and Ford
administrations.

When the Kennedy Center was completed, Jackie wrote, "All
passes, art alone endures" and wrote a description of the mission
for the center: "Washington has been our nation's capital for a

century and three-quarters. But only recently have we begun to understand that a great nation is nourished by art as well as politics. In other countries' capitals, cities have their theaters, opera houses and concert halls. But our capital city has lacked adequate space for our orchestras, singers, dancers and actors. Now, at last, we will have a home for the performing arts in our own nation's capital. Here there will be splendid productions of opera, music, theater, dance and films that will give our performing artists a national base and will strengthen artistic opportunities and standards throughout the land."

She reveals her deep commitment to the role of the arts center: "For the Kennedy Center exists not for Washington alone. It exists for the entire nation. Its work will be closely linked with state arts councils, municipal art centers, colleges, schools and museums everywhere in our country. I am particularly glad that provisions are being made to set aside a proportion of the tickets for every performance at special rates, to be reserved for students and seniors and those who are not able to pay the box office ticket. This is a place not just for the wealthy elite, but for all America."

President Kennedy once said: "If we can make our country one of the great schools of civilization like Athens in ancient Greece, then on that achievement will surely rest our claim to the ultimate gratitude of mankind . . . I am certain that after the dust of centuries has passed over our cities, we will be remembered not for victories or defeats in battle or in politics but for our contributions to the human spirit."

The Burden and the Glory, The Place of the Artist in Society, America the Beautiful, and *A Nation of Immigrants* were published after Kennedy's assassination in 1964. The Anti-Defamation League of B'nai B'rith originally published a pamphlet titled *A Nation of Immigrants* in 1958, and the expanded version includes a survey of the problems and the contributions of the various ethnic groups in America. *The Burden and the Glory* serves as the final volume of the trilogy of Kennedy speeches after *A Strategy for Peace* and *To Turn The Tide.* The true record of President John F. Kennedy, and the depth of his understanding of world politics are brilliantly described in these three volumes of speeches. The Kennedy administration's battle to achieve the following legislative accomplishments of the eighty-sixth and eighty-seventh Congress are described in a rigorous political fashion that distinguish his speeches with vitality and a profound determination: the Alliance for Progress in Latin America, the Nuclear Test Ban Treaty, the Civil Rights Act, the Peace Corps, a full-scale outer-space program designed to land a man on the moon in the mid-60's, the Educational Television Act that funded an expansion of public broadcasting television and he appointed Eleanor Roosevelt to head a Commission on the Status of Women. The trilogy of Kennedy's speeches is required reading for every American and for anyone who wants to be elected president.

"I look forward to an America which will not be afraid of grace and beauty . . . and I look forward to an America which commands respect throughout the world not only for its strength but for its civilization as well, " Kennedy observes in *America the Beautiful*. The Kennedy administration passed the first major additions to the National Park System since 1946. *America the Beautiful* explores the themes found in President Kennedy's introduction to Secretary of the Interior, Stewart Udall's book on conservation *The Quiet Crisis*. President Kennedy passed environment conservation legislation that included a fund for future land acquisition and the preservation of wilderness areas. Another bill passed doubled the water pollution prevention program, and established the first major control of air pollution. On September 15th, 1963, he spoke at the University of Wyoming: "One of the great resources which we are going to find in the next forty years is not going to be the land; it will be in the ocean . . ."

In 1962, Richard Nixon reported, "When I told Kennedy I was considering the possibility of joining the "literary ranks" of which he is himself so distinguished a member, he expressed the thought that every public man should write a book at some time in his life, both for mental discipline and because it tends to elevate him in popular esteem to the respected status of an "intellectual"."

Perhaps President Kennedy was having a little fun with a Republican wondering how to win a presidential race. Not long after that exchange, Nixon authored *Six Crises,* which won him the prestige that his 1960 presidential opponent had already achieved.

In 1963 the First Lady presided over the *Mona Lisa* exhibition, and many other notable dinners including the state dinner to honor the Grand Duchess and her son the Prince of Luxembourg. Jackie organized Basil Rathbone to recite Elizabethan poetry and music to entertain her guests. Her poetry selections included works by Shakespeare, Marlowe, Ben Jonson and John Donne. Jackie discovered a group of instrumentalists, the Consort Players, who performed on musical instruments from Shakespeare's era such as the virginal, cittern, trele viol, bass viol, flute, lute, and a variation of the bass guitar, a pandora.

On April 9th, 1963, Jackie and President Kennedy's lifelong admiration for Sir Winston Churchill inspired the ceremony to grant him an American citizenship. On June 23, Jackie, nearly six months pregnant, joined the President for her last official appearance before the birth of her son Patrick. At the state dinner for President Radhakrishnan of India, she invited the Opera Society of Washington to perform Mozart's *The Magic Flute.* She decided to spend her remaining summer months at the Kennedy family's Cape Code seashore estate. On August 6th, she was rushed to Otis Naval Base and gave birth by caesarean section. Baby Patrick suffered from a respiratory illness, and lived only two days. The death of that baby brought the Kennedy's together, they found solace in a stronger marital bond.

Her sister, Princess Lee Radziwill, suggested Jackie take a recuperative holiday as a guest of Aristotle Onassis in Greece, then travel to Morocco as a guest of King Hussein's. Before her departure, the first lady insisted on attending the welcoming ceremony at Union Station for the Emperor of Ethiopia. That evening Rose Kennedy acted as White House hostess at the state dinner for the Emperor, Halie Salassie on October 1, 1963.

Many years after her 1963 tour of Greece, one August evening in 1968 shortly before Jackie was to marry Aristotle Onassis, she gushed to her future sister-in-law Artemis, "I saw *Electra* performed at the site of the ancient Greek ruins. A wonderful actress, Anna Synodinou, played the title role and I was so impressed with her acting. I went up to her after her performance and remarked how amazed I was that someone so young as she could play such a role. She told me that she was not so young, but was the same age as *Electra*. I was amazed."

In late 1962, Eleanor Roosevelt died, and Jackie attended her funeral. President Kennedy commissioned the Eleanor Roosevelt commemorative stamp, and presented the final report of the President's Commission on the Status of Women. Mrs. Roosevelt was the head of that commission. He welcomed visits from Prime Minister Sean F. Lemass of Ireland, President Tito of Yugoslavia, and gave speeches to several audiences including the second conference on U.S. and Japanese cultural and educational exchange programs, the National Trust for Historic Preservation and those attending the dedication of Robert Frost's Library at Amhearst College. Most importantly, Kennedy was preparing for his re-election campaign in 1964, so he agreed to visit Texas to advance this cause.

In 1974, Jackie gave an oral history to The Johnson Library, observing, "he (JFK) was warned not to go by Senator Fulbright, Adlai Stevenson and Bobby, to whom they had given messages . . . Vice President Johnson would not agree to ride in the car with the President in Dallas. " President John F. Kennedy's assassination on November 22nd, 1963 sustained conspiracy theories that were proven and disproven and proven so many times suggests perhaps several conspiracies. The President's alleged assassin Lee Harvey Oswald was murdered by Jack Ruby, and this lost testimony may have sealed the truth in his grave. Jacqueline Kennedy, a mother left to raise two young children, once said of her husband. "He's a rock and I lean on him in everything. He gave me a raison d'etre."

"Very few people know what really lay behind the assassination in Dallas. Bobby Kennedy knew it all. The last time he came to Paris, he told me, 'Now it is my turn . . .'" Andre Malraux confides to his biographer Pierre Galante in 1971. "Between the Kennedy's and de Gaulle there is a joint bond. Going to Dallas for Kennedy, passing by the Petit-Clamart for de Gaulle meant the same sort of attitude. It is the knowledge that 'I must go' that de Gaulle shared with Kennedy." Malraux reflects that for both men history was much more important than their own lives, they were willing at any moment to sacrifice their lives. As a World War II hero, Andre Malraux lived his life on these terms as well.

Rose Fitzgerald Kennedy wrote in her book *Times To Remember*: "Ecclesiastes is one of my favorite Books of the Old Testament, as it was also for my son President John F. Kennedy. Some of these lines were read during his funeral services in 1963."

> *All things have their season, and in their time all things pass*
> *under heaven.*
> *A time to be born, and a time to die ;*
>   *a time to plant, and a time to pluck up that which is*
> *planted.*
> *A time to weep, and a time to laugh;*
>   *a time to mourn, and a time to dance.*
> *A time to get, and a time to lose;*
>   *a time to keep, and a time to cast away.*
> *A time to rend, and a time to sew;*
>   *a time to keep silence, and a time to speak . . .*

She continues, "For every man that eateth and drinketh, and seeth good of his labor, this is the gift of God . . . Nothing is better than for a man to rejoice in his work, and that this is his portion. For he shall bring him to know the things that shall be after him."

"I remember going over to the White House to ask President Johnson for two things." The former first lady said privately in her 1974 oral history interview on Lyndon Baynes Johnson. "One was to name the space center in Florida Cape Kennedy." Jackie's memory of her husband's speech in Texas about his plans to launch

the first rocket to the moon, was one of his dreams she feared for:
"That's going to be forgotten, and his dreams are going to be forgotten . . . maybe they'll remember that some day this man did
dream that." Her second wish was to continue the plans of the
Fine Arts Commission and the President's Advisory Council on
the Arts.

Jackie began her mission to keep her husband's memory alive:
"He changed our world, and I hope people will remember him all
their lives." If President Kennedy had survived, he planned to write
his autobiography, lecture on American politics, publish a national
newspaper and the most interesting possibility, returning to Congress as a Senator. As president, he was one of the most extensively
traveled men to enter the White House, so he would most likely
continue his adventures to gain first-hand knowledge about the
world to inspire his future writing. His popularity and desire to
inform the general public ranks him as the best teacher of modern
politics in America. When one explores Kennedy as a spectacular
man of politics, letters, and action, the facts surrounding Dallas
become banal and meaningless. It is truly of greater significance
that Kennedy's last interview published in *McCall's* in November
of 1963 was titled, "JFK: What Women Can Do for Peace Now".

"The early reports of the President's assassination were not
decisive . . . of the grim news that followed, I can only say that it
was a shattering sensation to discover quite abruptly that one had
lived the best year's of one's life . . ." one of Washington's most
trusted journalists since FDR's presidency Joseph Alsop reveals his
personal feelings: "I had never known I loved the president, for
one does not think of this kind of relationship in those terms,
until I felt the impact of his death. The fact is that Jack Kennedy
had an extraordinary knack for capturing people and changing
them. To me, this was his most inexplicable quality . . ."

The universe Kennedy inherited as president was faltering by
1960. But towards the end of 1963, he demonstrated an ability to
suppress Communism in Cuba, South America, and Laos, improve under-developed science and technology with a space

program, address violence and colonialism in Algeria and the chaos of racial hatred over the admission of James H. Meredith to the University of Mississippi. Joe Alsop recalls in his memoirs, "In my column that day, I paid tribute to John Kennedy as a man, 'perfectly formed to lead the United States of America,' who taking over the country in a time of violent change, had succeeded profoundly, 'only to be cut off before his task was half-done.'"

At the invitation of President Eamon de Valera, President John F. Kennedy toured Ireland in late June of 1963. On his way to Ireland from West Berlin he said, "It is that quality of the Irish, that remarkable combination of hope, confidence, and imagination that is needed more than ever today. Those who suffer in Berlin behind that wall of shame . . . let them remember the boys of Wexford who fought with heart and hand to burst in twain the galling chain and free their native land . . ." The final effects of the Fitzgerald-Kennedy politics in America are hard to define because each generation has effectively embraced new ideas and reformed aging political systems. Their leadership has unveiled old prejudices, and excellerated an American belief that all people are entitled to the same opportunities to improve their lives.

Benjamin Bradlee, his friend and longtime Georgetown neighbor remarked, "John Kennedy reveled in love for the Irish patrimony that he had left so far behind. He laughed with love at the roguery of his grandfather, Honey Fitz, and his trip to Ireland in 1963 was a pilgrimage to that love." When Kennedy quoted two prominent Irish writers James Joyce and George Bernard Shaw, the *Irish Times* reported that, "this was the first time the names of the great Irish novelists had been mentioned in the halls of Dublin's parliament, except in legislative arguments about censorship. The President quoted George Bernard Shaw's passage: "Other people see things and say why? But I dream of things that never were, and I say, why not?"

A JOURNEY TO CAMBODIA

Jacqueline Onassis told founder of *Ms.* magazine, Gloria Steinem, in 1979, "If I hadn't married, I might have had a life very much like Gloria Emerson's. She's a friend who started out in Paris writing about fashion, and then ended up as a war correspondent in Vietnam. The two ends of her life couldn't seem farther apart and that is the virtue of journalism. You never know where it's going to take you, but it can be a noble life." Jackie never wrote about the Vietnam War, but she was vehemently opposed to President Johnson's policy to accelerate American troop involvement after the death of her husband. President Kennedy's foreign policy in Southeast Asia inspired her 1967 journey to Cambodia to diffuse Prince Sihanouk's lingering anti-American sentiments. One of the American Ambassadors's staff members Anita Allegra said that "the pictures of Jackie's trip to Cambodia are all over the walls of the embassy, and the Prince is now King Sihanouk, who is also a musician and filmmaker," and greatly admired Jackie's love for diverse cultures.

"The problems created by the Pol Pot regime . . ." Anita Allegra laments, "people everywhere have stories of horror, and lost family members." The Cambodian people still suffer from the repercussions of the warfare during the Vietnam Wars and the holocaust that followed.

Anita Allegra was intrigued that Princess Norodom Bopha Dhevi, a former member of the Royal Cambodian Ballet, once met Jacqueline Kennedy. Prince Sihanouk's daughter, Princess

Norodom performed for Mrs. Kennedy on her 1967 visit. Allegra said, "That's interesting. Now, she's Cambodia's Minister of Culture."

The Kennedy administration's November 1963 foreign policy in Southeast Asia was devastated after the assassination of Vietnam leaders President Ngo Dinh Diem and his brother-in-law Counselor to the President Ngo Dinh Nhu. Prince Norodom Sihanouk of Cambodia severed diplomatic relations with the Kennedy White House suspecting U.S. participation in the deaths. Four years after the assassination of President Kennedy, Jacqueline Kennedy at the invitation of Prince Sihanouk, on the world's impression that she was acting as a Goodwill Ambassador to name a street after President John F. Kennedy, agreed to visit the ancient ruins of the Khmer civilization Angkor Wat in Cambodia.

International print and television news media covered Jacqueline Kennedy's trip to Cambodia. Reports of the Vietnam War appeared daily on the major networks. The former first lady, Jacqueline Kennedy, claimed to be fascinated with the Khmer history and ancient ruins of Angkor Wat. But the trip was organized by the United States State Department and it was later discovered Robert Kennedy hoped her visit would alleviate the American government's fractured diplomatic relations with Cambodia. Robert Kennedy was specifically concerned with Cambodia's involvement in the Vietnam conflict, and the American bombing of tiny villages.

As reported by Kenneth O'Donnell and Dave Powers in October of 1963, President Kennedy ordered to evacuate 1,000 military personnel and advisors so that by the end of 1965, the American Green Beret advisory force would be completely out of South Vietnam. Kennedy planned for ambassador-at-large Averell Harriman to negotiate a truce with the Communist regime in North Vietnam that reflected the agreements with Nikita Khrushchev in Laos in 1961. Kennedy's foreign policy supported South Vietnam's desire to remain independent, and to prevent North Viet Cong's Communist sponsored guerrilla attacks, so that the local population could peacefully chose its own future. In 1954 the Geneva

Accords divided the country at the 17th Parallel into a northern Communist territory ruled by Ho Chi Minh and the independent Republic of South Vietnam's government lead by Ngo Dinh Diem in Saigon. President Ngo Dinh Diem and his brother-in-law Nhu faced mounting terrorists attack as the aggressive Red Chinese guerrilla military units infiltrated Ho Chi Minh's Communist regime.

Kennedy argued that French forces fighting Vietnamese rebels, backed by the Red Chinese, and led by nationalist leader Ho Chi Minh were defeated in 1954. General Charles de Gaulle warned in their 1961 meetings in Paris, "After eight years of fighting an estimated 400,000 men had died in battle." The North Viet Cong terrorists attacks worsened in October of '63, when Diem's troops began raiding Buddhist pagoda's and the monks lit themselves on fire in protest. Madame Nhu's cruel television remarks, "on the barbecue show" sacrifice of "so-called holy men", ignited an American sentiment to call off all aid to Saigon. Kennedy appointed an Ambassador to Vietnam Henry Cabot Lodge, who opposed the Diem/Nhu regime. General Paul Harkin at the Pentagon, and others at the CIA believed that Ngo Dinh Diem was an honest and true nationalist in control of the sympathy of his people, and no other leader could be as effective. The conflicts between the presidency, the CIA, and the Pentagon created an air of distrust as the military 'agenda' regarding Vietnam was not a unified plan of action.

In September of 1963, journalist Joe Alsop realized that President Diem and Nhu were in serious political trouble when he revisited Saigon in South Vietnam. His private meetings with Nhu revealed Nhu had hatched a secret plan to conduct independent peace negotiations with Ho Chi Minh in Hanoi to end the Vietnam War. President Diem had not been advised of this plan. Alsop observes in his memoirs, "By 1963, President Diem was being maliciously and constantly traduced by the American newspapermen in Saigon. In my view, there is no more foolish fault, either in the newspaper profession or ordinary life, than to grow obsessed by the pimples of your friends . . . while forgetting the hideous ulcers of your enemies . . . This, it seems to me, is a peculiarly

American weakness. In China, Chiang Kai-shek may not have been the ideal moral man, but he most certainly was not the egomaniacal madman that Mao Tse-tung turned out to be ..." Alsop believed that any American loss in Southeast Asia would turn the balance of power so favorably in the direction of the Communists, that an American victory was imperative. Alsop apprised President Kennedy upon his return to Washington, but the news of the Diem/Nhu conflicts only hastened Kennedy's desire to evacuate American advisors.

The transcript of President John F. Kennedy's Recordings of White House Telephone Conversations indicate the severity of the confusion caused by an unstable American ally in Southeast Asia in late October of 1963:

October 2, 1963, 11:00a.m.:
Vietnam: President Kennedy reviews news coverage of Communist Viet Cong and American casualties, possible troop reduction, North Vietnamese supply difficulties, Madame Nhu's activities, news coverage of Lodge/CIA dispute, Ambassador to Vietnam Henry Cabot Lodge's position regarding Diem/Nhu Saigon government in South Vietnam and possible public statement.

October 5, 1963, 9:30a.m.:
Vietnam: President Kennedy reviews impact on government of Vietnam if United States cuts off commodities. The prevailing issues are most important, Vietnamese oppression of Buddhists, the Pentagon's General Paul Harkin meeting with Diem and Tung, Ambassador to Vietnam Henry Cabot Lodge's role, conditions needed for resumption of aid, General Harkin's role regarding military, proposed testimony before Congressional committee, beating of American journalists, Ambassador Lodge's protest to government of Vietnam and the timing of the reduction of U.S. troops and advisors.

October 8, 1963, 5:30p.m.:

Vietnam: President Kennedy reviews aid to Tung forces, aid programs and costs, defense budget, possible coup, use of Conein, U.S. position regarding coup, military display for Vietnamese Independence Day, Ambassador Lodge's location, McNamara/Taylor appearances before the Foreign Relations Committee.

October 25, 1963, 11:05a.m.:

Vietnam: President Kennedy reviews intelligence report on Vietnam, instructions for Ambassador Lodge . . . portions closed due to national security classification.

October 28, 1963:

Vietnam: President Kennedy reviews intelligence report on Vietnam, orientation of various Vietnamese forces, review of 1960 coup attempt, Ambassador Lodge to return to U.S. or not . . . chain of command.

October 30, 1963:

Vietnam: President Kennedy reviews drafting of message to Lodge, assessment of present situation, . . . chain of command.

November 1, 1963:

Vietnam: President Kennedy reviews report on military coup in Vietnam, constitutional government in Vietnam, and U.S. troop involvements.

November 2, 1963:

Vietnam: President Kennedy reviews assessment of coup in Vietnam, reports of deaths of Diem and Nhu, review of developments leading to coup, whether or not Ambassador Lodge should return to U.S. for briefing, restoration of constitutional government in Vietnam . . .

The American televisions networks and the press stationed in Vietnam exploited the news of Diem and Nhu's deaths and the horrifying brutality of guerrilla warfare in Vietnam. In the hearts of young Americans, the press redefined the mission of war so that it was no longer honorable soldiers dying in battlefields but American martyrs sent into a vast jungle of killing fields too foreign and terrifying to navigate.

"They want me to send combat units over there," the President said to Kenneth O'Donnell and Dave Powers in late October of 1963, "That means sending draftees, along with volunteer regular Army advisors into Vietnam. I'll never send draftees over there to fight." Four years later, Jacqueline Kennedy departed for Southeast Asia the week of November 17th, 1967. At the Pochentong Airport, from under a gold-tipped parasol, Prince Norodom Sihanouk bowed low, and a royal honor guard in sampots, the traditional baggy Cambodian trousers, stood at attention. The hatless, fragile and lovely tourist emerged from a United States Air Force plane. As she walked away from the ramp, two hundred Cambodian schoolgirls, carrying silver bowls, sprinkled the red carpet with rose and jasmine petals.

"You are receiving the honored Buddhist welcome for very special guests," the Prince murmured.

Jacqueline Kennedy and her host, His Royal Highness Prince Norodom Sihanouk, Chief of State of the Buddhist Kingdom of Cambodia walked through the blossoms and applause to a pair of gilded thrones, set up in the royal reception hanger and paused for photographers. They knew they were in the midst of a delicate and sensitive moment. Silence was suddenly golden and diplomatic, as the cameras captured the historic reunion of the Kennedy's and Cambodia.

The pomp which Sihanouk had ordered for Mrs. Kennedy's gilt-edged trappings was normally reserved for a visiting potentate of a great power rather than just another tourist, however charming. More important was the effect her visit had on the relations between the United States and Cambodia. She was, after all, being received with fanfare, by the chief of a nation with which her own country had no diplomatic relations.

The plan for the trip originated when W. Averell Harriman sent a letter via Robert Shaplen, the Southeast Asia correspondent for the *New Yorker*, to the Prince asking if he was still willing to receive Mrs. Kennedy.

The Prince responded with a personal letter written in French asking Jacqueline Kennedy to be present at the unveiling of a plaque commemorating the naming of 'Avenue John F. Kennedy' in the port city of Sihanoukville. All political motivations were submerged beneath Mrs. Kennedy's desire to explore the cultural landscape of Angkor Wat. It was simply that her presence in Cambodia and Prince Sihanouk's dedication of the Kennedy plaque were to be symbols of an improvement in relations.

As many knowledgeable observers suspected at the time, Jacqueline's trip was not just a casual visit. A journey of over ten thousand miles from her Fifth Avenue, New York City apartment to a remote Asian nation was obviously inspired by more than a desire to visit the ruins of Angkor to "fill a lifelong dream" as reported in her press statement. The long journey to the capital city of Phnom Penh presented many questions that the press would find conflicting with the reason for her six day visit.

Why was the widow of a United States President undertaking this long journey? Was it possible to believe she would leave her small children to go on a sight-seeing journey so far from home to a country caught in the cross-fire of the Vietnam War? Why would she agree to take part in a memorial ceremony to her husband in a small Cambodian city reported to be a supply port for Vietcong military arms and equipment, an American enemy? Why would she pay tribute to a memorial to her husband in a country that has

allegedly allowed the Vietcong and North Vietnam forces to oper-
ate bases inside his territory? As a private citizen why was she traveling on board an official United States Air Force plane? Why did
the highest government official receive her as if she were on a state
visit? Finally, Mrs. Kennedy's aloofness gave the impression that
she feared dropping a state secret or slipping in an unguarded
moment to the American and international press the true purpose
of her mission.

Only a selection of loyal Kennedy advisors sympathetic to a
foreign relations policy to de-escalate the Vietnam War knew that
her silences were calculated. Her high-level diplomatic trip was
later discovered to be a secret plan to restore the tiny nation's faith
in America's goal to negotiate a lasting peace in Southeast Asia.
Although Eleanor Roosevelt had performed many a diplomatic
service, never in American history had the wife of a former President been sent so far from home to an area so sensitive, to perform
a mission so delicate.

There was a sense of pageantry and history as Jacqueline and
her entourage arrived at the airport in Cambodia's capital. The
Ambassador from Great Britain to Kennedy's New Frontier David
Ormsby-Gore, Lord Harlech, and a trusted friend of President
Kennedy's, gave an air of proper protocol as her official escort.
Lord Harlech, like Jackie, recently lost his spouse, when his wife,
Sylvia, was killed in an automobile accident.

The other members of the party included; Michael V. Forrestall,
a former White House specialist on Vietnam, now in private law
practice. Special ambassador-at-large and peace negotiator, W.
Averell Harriman, and Mr. and Mrs. Charles Bartlett, the newspaper columnist who introduced John F. Kennedy to Jackie in 1951.

After the royal pomp and parade down the alley, the
Prince—Samdech Euv, or "Papa Prince" as 6,250,000 Cambo-
dians lovingly address him, introduced his guest to his personal family, political generals, the diplomatic corps, including the Australian and the Soviet ambassadors, but not the
Communist Chinese ambassador. The Prince seemed hopeful

to clear the air of vanquished dreams, determined to find success in Jackie's mission. The spectacular reunion marked a new beginning for his people, as they drove through the wide tropical streets of the capital city of Phnom Penh to the Khemarin Palace.

Jackie's international story began as if a modern day *King and I* revival. Staged among a kind of living bas-relief of ancient ruins, so unreal that the next six days continued to gather a momentous wonder as a tableaux of spectacular images captured the mystique of Cambodia's antiquity. Many a pilgrimage to Angkor has been celebrated in literature, Andre Malraux wrote about it in *The Royal Way*. But never before had the images of such a lovely awe-struck woman crossed so many magazines and television cameras creating an extraordinary visual tour de force that unleashed the passion both countries shared for peace in Southeast Asia.

Sihanouk, was publicly against American military involvement in the Vietnam War. He wished for the powerful Americans to stop bombing tiny Cambodia. In spite of his frustration with Washington, Jacqueline Kennedy was received like a honored diplomat. A gala dinner in Chamcar Mon Palace on the Mekong River was followed by a performance of the royal ballet. With white frangipani blossoms in her hair, Princess Bopha Devi, Sihanouk's stunningly beautiful daughter and star of the ballet, led ten dancers in a re-enactment of Cambodian legendary dance. Jackie in a lime green gown edged with silver to match her shoes, exchanged expressions of wonder in French and both seemed to enjoy the evening. In a toast, Sihanouk praised President Kennedy, "he lit a light that has never been relit and which we miss cruelly today."

Jackie gave the impression that she longed to immerse herself in the Khmer splendor of the past. Prince Sihanouk longed for his tiny kingdom to be respected among the world powers. Jacqueline seemed to be in search of an antiquity that would give her a moment of quiet reflection. While the Prince's remarks provoked the international media's headline answers behind his foreign policy to end the Vietnam War.

Their desires and plans inspired a mutual admiration as Jackie and the Prince agreed that the splendors of Cambodia's ancient culture was the perfect background to argue a case for peace. The ruins of Angkor made it all seem nonpolitical, a chance to exchange gifts and memories worthy of a lasting friendship. As more details surfaced, the nonpolitical side of the trip was planned to delicately divert the press from inflating bitter feelings by taking sides. Jackie's diplomatic mission was designed to avoid headlines regarding military intervention, in hopes to simply open communications between Phnom Penh and Washington D.C.

In October of 1967, after her journey was announced she received dozens of letters from families of American prisoners-of-war hopeful that she could inquire about the safety of their relations. Jackie wished to help in some way, but Harriman firmly regarded her trip as an opening for possible future requests. He sensed that right-wing criticism may cause a serious snafu in her plans to visit 'leftist' Cambodia. It seemed best not to engage in serious diplomatic business, but to limit her activities to showing the flag and her famous American smile.

Senator Robert Kennedy was consulted and expressed concern for the welfare of two American civilians captured by the Vietcong may provide some relief for the release of military prisoners-at-war. The two civilians were Gustuv C. Hertz and Douglas K. Ramsey. Sadly, Hertz's death was announced while Mrs. Kennedy was in Cambodia. This shocked her so deeply, that she broke diplomatic instructions and pleaded with Prince Sihanouk to use his personal influence with the Vietcong to assure the well-being of all American prisoners-of-war. He was compassionate but noncommittal.

The sojourn reflected the complexity of foreign relations among the nations engaged in the Vietnam War. There seemed to be no clear distinction among a division of loyalties, only mounting deaths, bombing of peasant villages and irreversible chaos in a region besieged for centuries by battles for political power and territory.

Her entourage boarded a government DC-3 and flew from Phnom Penh to the plains of Siem Reap. She arrived just in time for the press corps to greet her arrival. The Cambodian government had handed down an edict permitting forty-five minutes for the press to take pictures, and requesting time to allow Mrs. Kennedy to meditate among the ruins in "calm absolu". All newsmen were barred from her three day tour. "This measure is taken at the express demand of Madame Kennedy!" the press statement announced. The Prince, a gentleman, even refused to disturb his guest, as he disclosed to his nation, "She told me that she wants to go to Angkor to meditate because she is a widow who keeps alive memories of her husband. The press should not disturb this great lady." Thus Jacqueline Kennedy's communion with the majestic Angkor civilization was a peaceful moment for reflection.

French archaeologist and curator of the Angkor monuments, Bernard Groslier, and her Cambodian hosts arranged a picnic lunch under tall hardwood trees, while a charming band of tiny gongs, cymbals and bamboo flutes carried soft sounds of music. That evening, the soaring sights of the six hundred temples at Angkor Wat, the best known of the Khmer temples, were illuminated by candles, torches and floodlights. Strolling barefoot through the shadows, Jackie paused to run her fingers over the stone friezes that depicted the ancient battles between gods and men.

Jacqueline's final plans included the dedication and naming of a street in honor of her husband "Avenue John F. Kennedy" in the port city of Sihanoukville. Then she would travel back through Thailand to dine with the King and the Queen. At the dedication, Jacqueline objected to an advance copy of Sihanouk's press statement, but the Prince staged three hours of protesting the Vietnam War. He unequivocally supported Hanoi's terms for ending the war in Viet Nam and argued that if Kennedy had lived, the war would have never reached the current proportions. Sihanouk was deliberate when he stated, "As soon as America stopped sending planes over the Cambodian border, barbarous bombings of civilians, and recognized his country's "territorial integrity" he would be delighted to resume diplomatic relations with Washington." Jacqueline replied that, "President Kennedy would have wished to visit Cambodia. He would have been attracted by the vitality of the Khmer people."

To the officials who organized "Jackie's sojourn", as Prince Sihanouk later referred to it, the mission was a graceful success. With the Prince, Jacqueline returned to Phnom Penh, to stage a feeding of the royal elephants, exchange gifts and tour the damage caused by the war. She was respectful and her visit seemed to have opened discussions for improved relations between Washington and Cambodia. Before Jackie left Cambodia, she offered Prince Norodom Sihanouk a talisman from the past, President Kennedy's collection of Senate speeches on foreign policy, *A Strategy For Peace*. Then the Kennedy party bid adieu to the Kingdom of Cambodia and departed for Thailand to spend three days of private sight-seeing.

The tense moments in Cambodia were replaced by casual shopping in Thailand. Jackie found a 15th century bronze Buddha, two 17th century gilt wooden hands, three porcelain cosmetic jars from the ruined capital city of Ayutthaya and three solid silver bracelets made by Thailand's Meo hill tribesman.

The high point of her Thai sojourn, an occasion that united two of the world's best dressed women, was a royal dinner for one hundred and eighty given by King Bhumibol and Queen Sirikit. Jackie wore a long white evening gown elaborately stitched in gold of Thai embroidered silk and the Queen wore a traditional gown of Thai embroidered silk in yellow with a matching sabai, a Thai stole.

After dinner, the King and Queen suggested that they take a little walk. Jacqueline particularly wanted to see the temple of the Emerald Buddha. The King had ordered the palace grounds and the temple to be illuminated. Lights shone on the golden spires and the gilded heads of the king cobras and demons that guard the temple including the white monkey king warrior and the life size golden statue of Manohra, a god of half human and half bird. Jackie called the temple, "the most beautiful thing I have ever seen."

She returned to the states via Rome. The international news reported the Cambodian government's opposition to the Vietnam War and American involvement. Jacqueline Kennedy hoped that her visit would accelerate the United States' peace negotiations in Southeast Asia. She was opposed to the escalating Vietnam War and Prince Sihanouk admired the Kennedy's compassion. He felt honored that Mrs. Kennedy was determined to show his country that she opposed the escalating warfare, and cared enough to travel so far from her home and her children.

Senator Robert Kennedy agreed with Prince Sihanouk and stated, "To the Vietnamese, however, it must often seem the fulfillment of the prophecy of Saint John the Divine: 'and I looked, and beheld a pale horse: and his name that sat on him was Death, and Hell followed with him. And power was given unto them over the fourth part of the earth, to kill with sword, with hunger and with death.'" Robert Kennedy remarked that, "wise policy is a setting of priorities, differentiating between that which is merely important and that which is truly essential . . . and it would be both callous and self-indulgent for those of us who sit comfortably at home to form policy without full knowledge and consciousness of the cost to others . . ."

In the midst of campaigning for the presidency, Robert Kennedy was shocked by the violent and sudden murder of Reverend Martin Luther King, Jr. Reverend King was elected president of both the National Association for the Advancement of Colored People (NAACP), and the Southern Christian Leadership Conference (SCLC). Reverend King, vehemently opposed to the human rights violations during the Vietnam War, was awarded a Nobel Peace Prize in 1964 for his international leadership during the Civil Rights Movement. Robert, Ethel and Jackie joined the King family in Atlanta to mourn his death. The depth of Martin Luther King's legacy is best measured by the emotional reaction of outrage in America and sympathy for the black community around the world.

In May of 1968, just six months after Jackie's visit to Cambodia,

Robert Kennedy, accepted the Democratic Presidential primary "so it's on to Chicago and let's win there . . ." His staff watching the televised speech heard floods of applause, and set off to greet the candidate at a discotheque, The Factory, for the post-primary party. Eight gunshots blasted on television, and behind the cameras, Rafer Johnson, Bill Barry and George Plimpton battled through the crowd to where Ethel was kneeling over Bobby. Ethel's voice, "Give him some air!" shot into the angry mob, while Rosie Grier held a man thought to be the killer, Sirhan Sirhan. Lee Radziwill called Jackie from London to find out if Bobby was alive, and Jackie immediately flew to Los Angeles to console Ethel. Jackie, behind the scenes, supported Ethel's wish that Leonard Bernstein's New York Philharmonic perform Gustav Mahler's Fifth Symphony and her old friend Andy Williams sing the 'Battle Hymn of the Republic' for Bobby's Requiem Mass at St. Patrick's Cathedral. The triple assassinations in America terrified Jackie, increasing her perception of possible danger to herself and her children.

"We have been stunned by the tragic death of Senator Robert Kennedy," Prince Norodom Sihanouk's message to Ethel Kennedy dated June 6, 1968 expressed his profound sadness, "and we beg you, Madame, to accept for yourself and for your children our deep condolences and sympathy for the cruel tragedy befalling you. The Cambodian people, and I myself wish to express our admiration to the Kennedy family whose sacrifices in the cause of peace, justice and liberty for the oppressed must not be in vain." Prince Norodom Sihanouk offers to meet the terms of Senator Robert Kennedy's request made just six months earlier: "In homage to the memory of the deeply regretted deceased, Cambodia desires to free without hesitation the two American soldiers interned for a violation of our territory."

What followed in Cambodia, the war during the sixties, the anti-Vietnamese pogroms of 1972, and the Pol Pot regime, was a variation of an age-old theme: genocide. In 1990, a friend of Jackie's, the French photographer, Marc Riboud, photographed hundreds of monks and thousands of pilgrims celebrating the three day festival to honor Buddha, rekindling a tradition extinguished during the years of persecution. In Buddhist Cambodia, amidst the memory of violence, one wonders how does the stone Buddha, savoring in his heart a peace that is Nirvana, smile with closed eyes?

BECOMING A BOOK EDITOR

After the assassination of Robert Kennedy, Jackie married the Greek shipping tycoon, Aristotle Onassis. She continued her work in New York City, joining the Municipal Art Society, protesting the demolition of the Metropolitan Opera House, supporting exhibitions at The Metropolitan Museum of Art, and raising funds to establish a permanent location for The International Center for Photography. Onassis hoped to create a sanctuary for his new wife to recover from the terrible nightmare of both JFK and RFK's deaths. With Onassis she traveled to Egypt on a sight-seeing tour, then invited famed Pop artist Andy Warhol to an exhibition of Egyptian antiquities at The Brooklyn Museum. Her life seemed to be busy, and focused on her children who gave her the greatest joy of all.

Life with Onassis included five years of entertaining on the *Christina*, and sadly more tragedies. When Aristotle Onassis' only son, Alexander, died in a plane accident, Onassis was inconsolable, the marriage suffered, and the couple entered into divorce proceedings. Onassis' death precipitated the divorce, and Jackie inherited approximately twenty-six million dollars. Once again, her life had taken a sudden turn, she was forty-four years old, and decided to look for a career rather than another husband. The Onassis years were a renewal. She emerged more mature and independent, and her inheritance created a rare freedom to enter the next phase of her life, becoming a book editor.

"I majored in literature, I had many friends in publishing, I love books, I've known writers all my life." She said that these were the 'obvious reasons' why she pursued a career as a book editor. She also admired photographers, performing artists and had a long association with talented people, any one of their stories could produce an interesting book.

In May of 1998, Jackie's publisher Marly Rusoff offered some direction in selecting which one of Jackie's forty authors to interview for the documentary film *Jackie: Behind the Myth*. Both her suggested authors, Peter Sis and Edvard Radzinsky were perfect. Marly Rusoff said, "Jackie cared very much about people's civil rights and individual freedoms, Russian, French, African American, and women's rights." Jackie edited *Taming the Storm* by Jack Bass, Michael Jackson, Judith Jamison and Dorothy West's book *The Wedding*." Judith Jamison danced in the opening performance of Leonard Bernstein's Mass at The Kennedy Center, and Jackie followed her career. Andre Previn, Louis Auchincloss and *The Paris Review's* George Plimpton were selected because their unique legacies added depth to American culture. Louis Auchincloss' appeal is formidable, as an American writer he has sustained a remarkable career for over forty years. Sadly some magnificent artists, including George Balanchine and Martha Graham, are alive spiritually, but mortally extinguished. After *Jackie: Behind the Myth's* principal photography, Andre Previn was awarded a Kennedy Center Honors in 1998, and then Judith Jamison was honored in 1999.

George Plimpton, who holds the self-appointed office of Fireworks Commissioner in New York City, recalls the genesis of his book, *Fireworks: A History and Celebration* commissioned by Jackie. George tells the story, "She saw the fireworks display out her window, and I had lunch with her the next day. 'My God, I saw the most beautiful fireworks show last night.' I said, 'well, you know, I was responsible for that, Jackie. Those were Chinese fireworks to celebrate Diana Vreeland's costume institute show.' She said, 'Well, they were the most beautiful things. Why don't we—you—you do a book on fireworks.' I said, 'Nobody will ever want to do a book on fireworks.' And so we talked about it for a while. And, that was what impressed me. I suddenly knew, I suddenly realized that Jackie could do anything she wanted."

Only one very feminine biography titled *Jacqueline Bouvier Kennedy* evokes Jackie's humor, impeccable breeding and quiet grace. Her friend Mary Van Rensselaer Thayer was granted the only chance to write the first lady's story with her cooperation. The book evolved from Van Rensselaer Thayer's articles that appeared in *Ladies Home Journal*. Jackie's editorial voice hints at her shy, yet also seductive maternal glamour, and the style of the writing elucidates her charm and manners. Whatever history that book fails to describe, it feels like Jackie, as if all her delicate intrigue and benevolence is staring out at the reader. George Plimpton remembers her aura: "She didn't have the persona to be a public figure, in a funny way. Although, she had the great beauty. Her voice was wrong for it. That high, strange whisper. But she always looked you right straight in the eye. It was amazing. And I think that was part of it, it's was like being in a cocoon."

In 1964, Jackie and Robert Kennedy selected the historian William Manchester to write *The Death of A President*, and granted the author extensive interviews. Almost immediately, she regretted her testimony and by January 16, 1967 she set in motion a notorious lawsuit to halt the publication of the book. William Manchester recalls when the whole affair became a media circus: "A friend phoned me from *Look* and read me a statement which had just been issued in Jackie's name. It accused me and my publishers of disregarding "accepted standards of propriety and good faith," of violating, "the dignity and privacy my children that I have striven with difficulty to retain," and of writing, "a premature account of the events of November 1963 that is in part both tasteless and distorted." Her rage and fury exploded with, "I am shocked that Mr. Manchester would exploit the emotional state in which I recounted my recollections to him in early 1964." Manchester concluded that the true explanation was that Jacqueline Kennedy didn't want any book to be published on the death of her husband, she simply wanted to forget all the painful memories. Edna

St. Vincent Millay once wrote about farewells: "Where you used to be, there is a hole in the world, which I find myself constantly walking around in the day-time and falling into at night. I miss you like hell."

After that experienced, she no longer openly supported any book on herself or John F. Kennedy. In 1974, she granted an interview to President Johnson's library, remained silent for over thirty years, and then at the request of Doubleday, agreed to give *Publisher's Weekly*, John F. Baker a long discussion about her experience as a book editor. John Baker recalled that in the publishing world, she was a respected and admired professional.

Jackie's friends share deep feelings about the role of the artist in society and her ability to inspire artistic excellence. She deeply admired Isaac Stern for his contributions as America's leading violinist, and his White House performance for Andre Malraux in 1962. Isaac Stern, Leonard Bernstein, John Steinbeck joined a distinguished group of artists as advisors on President Kennedy's innovative Advisory Council on the Arts. Isaac Stern's salvation of one of America's finest concert halls Carnegie Hall from demolition is a wonderful story of inspired architectural preservation. Both George Balanchine and Isaac Stern have been awarded the impressive French Legion of Honor, the French Commander of the Order of Arts and Letters decoration and National Institute of Arts and Letters award for Distinguished Service to the Arts. On the Kennedy marriage, Isaac Stern observes, "Well, she and he loved language. She loved the visual arts. He loved the intellectual part of the arts. Together they make a great combination."

Isaac Stern's vision of the arts in America and his ability to communicate his ideas paralleled President Kennedy and Jackie's: "I was there one day visiting Pierre Salinger, as he had arranged for me to see the President. Kennedy came over and said, 'Well Isaac you're going to argue for the arts again today?' I said yes, so he laughed and we sat down."

Isaac Stern recalls, "We discussed the possibility of creating a cabinet position for the arts. I was thinking of the secretary of culture that later became the National Endowment for the Arts and Humanities. All that was on track with Mrs. Kennedy. She instinctively felt the need for the arts. She knew that ballet, music, literature, and painting were part of what we call a civilized life."

Jacqueline Kennedy wished to bring to America the legacy of European culture and traditions, as a way to expand American interest in supporting art in general. Shakespeare was performed just once in 1910 for President Taft on the White House lawn. Knowing that President Ferik Ibrahim Abboud of the Sudan enjoyed Shakespearean drama, on October 4, 1961, Mrs. Kennedy invited the American Shakespeare Festival Theatre of Stratford, Connecticut to perform readings and scenes from its repertory. Mrs. Kennedy's former professor of English at Vassar, Helen Sandison, was invited as an honored guest. Jackie felt that her professor had inspired the evening's program long ago through thoughtful instruction in a classroom.

The performance included the prologue from *Henry V*, the murder of Duncan as the drunken-porter scene from *Macbeth*; the *"Seven Ages of Man"* speech from *As You Like It*; a scene from *Troilus and Cressida*; and as the finale, Prospero's soliloquy from *The Tempest*.

> *Our revels now are ended. These our actors,*
> *As I foretold you, were all spirits and*
> *Are melted into air, into thin air:*
> *And, like the baseless fabric of this vision,*
> *The cloud-capp'd towers, the gorgeous palaces,*
> *The solemn temples, the great globe itself,*
> *Yes, all which it inherit, shall dissolve*
> *And, like this insubstantial pageant faded,*
> *Leave not a rack behind. We are such stuff*
> *As dreams are made on, and our little life*
> *Is rounded with a sleep.*

Isaac Stern observes, "It was an instinct she had. It was a regal instinct and that's something that so few people have. And it knows its own value without saying anything. There was such a natural warm graciousness about her. You know people don't learn elegance, they either have it or they don't. She had it. She was a necessary figure around whom all the good thoughts could coalesce."

When she first became a book editor in 1979, Gloria Steinem interviewed the former First Lady on her professional life in an article titled "Why Does This Woman Work?" Jacqueline Onassis quotes Edith Hamilton in her description of the path to happiness: "The exercise of vital powers along lines of excellence in a life affording them scope, is an old Greek definition of happiness." This was a favorite passage of her husband, John F. Kennedy.

Some of her early projects at Viking Press included Muffie Brandon's history book *Remember The Ladies: Women in America, 1750-1815*, Eugene Kennedy's biography of Mayor Daley *Himself*, and Nancy Zaroulis' novel *Call The Darkness Light*. The history volume *Remember The Ladies* was inspired by Abigail Adam's plee to her husband John Quincy Adams during the early stages of forming the American government. The entire quote is the following: "By the way of the new Code of Laws which I suppose it will be necessary for you to make I desire you would Remember The Ladies, and be more generous and favorable to them than your ancestors. Do not put such unlimited power into the hands of the Husbands. Remember all men would be tyrants if they could be. If particular care and attention is not paid to the Ladies we are determined to foment a Rebellion, and will not hold ourselves bound by any Laws in which we have no voice or Representation. That your Sex are Naturally Tyrannical is a Truth so thoroughly established as to admit of no dispute, but such of you who wish to be happy willingly give up the harsh title of Master for the more tender and endearing one of Friend."

When Viking Press published a novel depicting the assassination of a character that resembled Ted Kennedy, Jackie left the firm for Doubleday. Nancy Tuckerman, Jackie's former White House social secretary, was a marketing executive at Doubleday, and felt Jackie would be 'safe' there. Nancy Tuckerman describes Jackie's employment, "It was strictly all business when she went to Doubleday as an Associate Editor. There was no preferential treatment. She worked out of a small, windowless office, and was committed to editing about twelve books a year." As many authors attest, with Jackie as their editor, it was they who were on the receiving end of the preferential treatment.

Around this time, her friend Karl Katz offered to act as her tour guide to Israel for the dedication of the Diaspora Museum in Tel Aviv. Karl Katz was the inspiration behind the museum. He observed she needed no instruction in the scriptural continuity from Old Testament to the New Testament. She planted a tree in Israel's John F. Kennedy Memorial Forest, visited a kibbutzim, and they explored biblical sites together. As the head of The Metropolitan Museum of Art's Film and Television Office, he became one of her close cultural allies. She supported Karl's hope to expand filming documentaries about the ancient stories of cultural enlightenment to be broadcast on PBS. After Karl gave her Larry Gonick's manuscript for *The Cartoon History of the Universe*, she published Volume I. The 'history' book was so successful that a second cartoon history book was commissioned and both are still in print.

Throughout her career, she remained interested in the lives of other women and commissioned biographies of movie star goddesses, Jean Harlow and Clara Bow. David Stenn authored both books, *Clara Bow: Runnin' Wild* and *Bombshell: The Life and Death of Jean Harlow*. Clara Bow, the legendary "It" Girl, was Hollywood's first sex symbol in the Roaring Twenties. A natural actress, she starred in one smash hit after another from 1922 to 1933, while the Hollywood machinery callously exploited her personal life. David Stenn's book sparked a new appreciation for the silent screen goddess, Clara Bow, the wild girl from Brooklyn. Stenn reported that, "I felt like I had an amazing, really cool, mother and an editor. It was great."

History, art and culture, areas of humanity both President Kennedy and Jackie shaped with carnal knowledge, gave every reason why the history of women was a natural area of interest for Jackie. Louis Auchincloss, with a troubled look, said, "I also wrote *False Dawn: Women in the Age of the Sun King.* Yes, there was a moment in history during the reign of Louis XIV, Jackie's favorite king, you know, when as many great women ruled as men. I thought that the independence of these women would lead to greater emancipation, but it was a false dawn." A cousin by marriage and a best-selling novelist, Louis Auchincloss described how he discovered the private diary of his wife's Vanderbilt grandmother, Adele Sloan, and "Jackie admired her strength of character and wanted to edit the memoirs." The history, recalling Adele Sloan's charmed life as she holds court in fantasy family estates, one for each season, unveiled that all was not well in even the wealthiest stratagems of American life. In her memoirs, titled *Maverick in Mauve,* Louis Auchincloss recounts the frustrating combination of the upper class women's 'educated artistic breeding' and the suffocation of her intelligence and limited opportunities in American life before women won the right to vote.

The performing arts, especially dance and ballet, are explored in autobiographies by Judith Jamison, Gelsey Kirkland and Martha Graham. Judith Jamison, Alvin Ailey's muse and Agnes de Mille's protege was coaxed by Jackie to co-author her memoirs titled *Dancing Spirit.*

Judith Jamison, the Artistic Director of the Alvin Ailey American Dance Theatre, maintains a reverence for Ailey that was recognized when Leonard Bernstein commissioned Ailey to choreograph the dance to accompany the music for *Mass.* Judith Jamison danced in the opening performance of *Mass* in 1971 to celebrate the first performance at The John F. Kennedy Center for Performing Arts.

The title of her book references her mentor Agnes de Mille, who Judith once said was, "the dancing spirit." Agnes de Mille discovered Judith in Philadelphia and invited her to New York to guest dance with the Ballet Theater. Judith recalls, "Agnes taught a master class in Philadelphia that surprised me because it didn't involve so much dancing as attitude. And then later I was to find out that she was full of attitudes. She was quite a remarkable woman. I smile because I remember her rambunctiousness. I loved her dancing energy." Agnes De Mille once said, "The truest expression of a people is in its dances and its music."

Jacqueline Onassis supported the Alvin Ailey American Dance Theatre, and she especially admired the ballet Judith Jamison choreographed as an homage to Alvin Ailey titled *Hymn*. "I was delighted that she understood how important the ballet was to the anniversary of our company. When she came backstage after the premiere of the ballet, she said something in French, that finished with "homage", and I just hung on that homage."

Dancing Spirit explores Judith's early influences from the dignity of her own parents and family to the African-American ballet teachers who held firm in the face of a segregated world. "I just come from a legacy of very strong women so Jacqueline Onassis can join the ranks there. I come from a line of women that are powerful although they have different statures in their lives, they're still powerful. When you have that kind of undeniable strength, then you really do believe that God doesn't give you any more than you can handle."

Gelsey Kirkland's two books *Dancing On My Grave* and *The Shape of Love* chronicle the delicate public impressions of the art of ballet as a behind the scenes competitive sport that crushes those who fail to maintain a personal equilibrium and sense of individuality. In brutal honesty, Kirkland warns in *Dancing On My Grave*: "I embarked on a risky course of plastic surgery, major dental realignments and gruesome medical procedures. I pray that young dancers, those who imitate me at their peril, will avoid this blind alley. It is more than a dead end; it is a dead beginning."As a long time board member of the American Ballet Theatre (ABT), Jacqueline Onassis caused a minor controversy when she announced that Gelsey Kirkland planned to author her debilitating experience as a celebrated ABT ballerina. *Dancing On My Grave* became a number one best-seller, revealing a long overdue examination of the pressures and the pitfalls of the high stakes ballet world.

"Dance is the hidden language of the soul." Martha Graham told the New York *Times* in 1985. The publication in 1991 of *Blood Memory* the autobiography of dancer and choreographer Martha Graham, (1894 to 1991) captures the innovative philosophy of the central figure of the modern dance movement. "Many times I hear the phrase the "dance of life." It is an expression that touches me deeply, for the instrument through which the dance speaks is also the instrument through which life is lived, the human body."

In more than one hundred and eighty dances created during a career of over fifty years, Martha Graham developed an original technique involving the expression of primal emotions through stylized bodily movement of great intensity. "It is through this, a great curiosity, that the legend's of the soul's journeys are retold with all their tragedy, and their bitterness and the sweetness of living . . . And there is grace. I mean the grace resulting from faith . . . faith in life, in love, in people, in the act of dancing. All this is necessary to any performance in life which is magnetic, powerful, rich in meaning."

Martha Graham started dancing in 1916 with Ruth St. Denis' modern dance company 'Denishawn' in Los Angeles, she debuted as the Priestess of Isis. She began her independent career in 1926 in New York City. Initially, Martha Graham was an enigma, but by 1937 she expressed a mystical new vision of American dance. "I danced at the White House in a little garden that was filled with flowers for the first time for President and Eleanor Roosevelt." She was later invited to dance there for seven other presidents . . . "when it was time to meet President Roosevelt, an usher said to me, 'You will not meet the President of the United States barefoot.'"

Introducing innovative stage design into her repertoire with a set created by Isamu Noguchi for her 1935 solo dance Frontier, Graham began a collaboration with the sculptor that lasted for three decades. "A curious intimacy exists between artists in collaboration. From the start, there was an unspoken language between Isamu and me. Our working together might have as its genesis as a myth, a legend, a piece of poetry, but there always emerged for me something of strange beauty and an otherworldliness." Noguchi designed close to twenty sets for Martha Graham, including those for her series based on Greek myths: Cave of the Heart (1946), Errand into the Maze (1947), Night Journey (1947), Clytemnestra (1958), Alcestis (1960), Phaedra (1962), Circe (1963) and Cartege of Eagles (1966). Graham also addressed Biblical and religious themes in other works for which Noguchi created sets, including Herodiade (1944), Judith (1950), Seraphic Dialogue (1955) and Embattled Garden (1958). She was awarded the Medal of Freedom from President Ford and a Kennedy Center Honors. Martha Graham never 'retired', but she no longer performed as a dancer after 1970, continuing to teach her dance technique and to choreograph for her company. Jackie supported Martha Graham's dance company and as the editor of Blood Memory recognized that her contribution to modern dance was unchallenged.

Andre Previn wrote his Hollywood memoirs No Minor Chords: My Days In Hollywood after Jackie urged him to send her a chapter. Like her many friendships with composers and conductors, Jackie marveled at Previn's talents: "She attended several concerts of mine and she liked coming to the New York Philharmonic when I conducted. I think her taste in music was quite conservative, Mozart and Haydn, Beethoven, Brahms. Maybe she had great floods of tears with Mahler, but I wasn't there to witness that. She did seem very taken with going to concerts and listening to music. As opposed to the royal family in England who go because they're supposed to go."

Born in 1928, Previn arrived in Los Angeles as a ten year old German refugee in 1939. A classically trained musician, he started hanging around the studios to make some extra money. In 1958, *Gigi* won Best Picture, Vincent Minelli won Best Director, Frederic Lowe for music, Alan Jay Lerner for lyrics and Andre Previn won the Oscar for best composer. It was the same year Bugs Bunny won the Irving Thalberg Award. 1959 was the year that virtually the only award *Ben-Hur* did not win was for best score which went to Andre Previn for *Porgy and Bess*. In 1963, he scooped up best musical score adaptation for *Irma La Douce*. By 1964 he had conquered Hollywood, and met as he remarked, "the only women who could give Jackie a run for the money . . . Audrey Hepburn." It was a big year for Julie Andrews' *Mary Poppins* and Audry Hepburn's *My Fair Lady* and Andre Previn won for *My Fair Lady's* musical score adaptation. He was nominated thirteen other times for a wide range of pictures including *Jesus Christ Superstar*. Previn discovered, in the nadir of success, that Hollywood's turgid culture became unbearably bombastic. He left for New York to refashion his life as an orchestral conductor and composer.

"Before my time at the studio," Previn told this funny story to Jackie, "MGM was run by a very famous wunderkind called Irving Thalberg. He ran a first cut of a big new drama in his projection room with all his minions around. There was something in the music that he didn't like. He said into this dark room, into his flock of people, 'What is that in the music that just happened, I hated that, what was that?' One of his people said, 'That was a minor chord Mr. Thalberg.' Thalberg said, 'Fine, I want to dictate a memo.' He dictated a memo that said from the above date on, no MGM picture will have a minor chord in it. And signed it. The memo was framed by the music librarian and instead of being hung on the wall, it was bolted with screws through the frame."

Previn told Jackie, "It was an inimitable piece of nostalgia. When I finally left MGM, I must say I came with a screwdriver, I was determined, but it had been locked in twenty-five years and I couldn't budge the screws, which made me very sorry. I thought that 'no minor chords' would be not a bad title. And there again, some people up at the publishing house objected to it because they said it would take too much explaining. She said, 'No, that's a wonderful title, leave it alone.'"

Merchant Ivory's screenwriter Ruth Prawer Jhabvala won the Oscar twice for screenplay adaptation, *A Room With a View* in 1986 and again in 1992 for *Howard's End*. In 1993, her novel *Poet and Dancer* was published by Doubleday, and Jackie was the editor. "The strength she exuded and put at the disposal of her authors came from her own vulnerability: she was aware of how you felt because she felt it herself . . . I was looking forward more than anything to our second book together . . ."

Jack Valenti, a Texan, and perhaps the closest aide to Lyndon Johnson during the Kennedy and Johnson administrations, departed in May of 1966 to become the long-standing head of the Motion Picture Association of America. He is the major duomo who has the final cut in ratings for every American movie. He once wrote of historian Thomas Babington Macaulay in the *Saturday Review*: "For uncounted millions of the untaught who awaken at the stirrings of sound and melody, who rise and enliven, at the unfolding of the human drama, there needs to be a Macaulay who touches them, and makes them eager and frequent visitors into the world of books." His first memory of Jackie was, "I met her on the last night of her husband's life . . . we shared a flight on Air Force One to Washington in the wake of a grotesque nightmare . . . so unexplainable, that the country was never again as it once was." *Protect and Defend* was his first novel, and as both an editor and a human being, he describes her as, "incapable of either a mean or graceless gesture. She was a loving friend."

Jackie worked with Jann Wenner, the founder of *Rolling Stone* magazine to create the collection of articles titled: *The Best of Rolling Stone: 25 Years of Journalism on the Edge.* Sarah Giles, authored a book titled *Fred Astaire: His Friends Talk.* There is no Academy Award category for film choreography, but if there was, Astaire's 1949 Honorary Oscar would have been named for his sphinx like dancing in dozens of films. She encouraged her friend from the White House years, and one of America's finest journalists, Bill Moyers, to adapt his television programs *Healing and the Mind, The World of Ideas I and II* and *The Power of Myth* into book editions. Bill Moyers cautioned the enthusiastic editor that he didn't believe there was a book in the television program. She prevailed and all the Moyers' volumes became best-sellers. Bill Moyer's introduced Jackie to the novelist Elizabeth Crook and Jackie edited two of her novels, *The Raven's Bride* and *Promised Lands*.

In July of 1963, President John F. Kennedy's Secretary of the Interior Stewart Udall wrote a forward to a collection of articles *The Quiet Crisis* discussing the conservation of natural resources in America and the concept of a land ethic. Thomas Jefferson, Teddy Roosevelt, FDR, Frederick Law Olmstead and numerous others fervently expressed the necessity and concern for the American tradition of land preservation, national parks and as Secretary Udell wrote, "men must grasp completely the relationship between human stewardship and the fullness of the American earth." President Kennedy added, "To this effort Secretary Stewart Udall has given his courageous leadership . . . *The Quiet Crisis* makes a stirring and illuminating contribution." In 1987, Jackie published Stewart Udall's *To The Inland Empire: Coronado and Our Spanish Legacy* a compilation of his essays describing the 1540 expedition of Conquistador Francisco Vasquez de Coronado's quest to find the "golden cities" of Cibola by tracking the southwestern geography of ancient Indian trails. Jerry Jacka's photographs of Mexico, Arizona and New Mexico reveal a noble American landscape as ancient as the temples at Abu Simbel.

In the 1994 interview Jackie granted to editorial director of *Publisher's Weekly* John F. Baker, she describes the kinds of books she admires: "I am drawn to books that are out of our regular experience. Books of other cultures, ancient histories. I'm interested in the arts in general, especially the creative process. I'm fascinated by hearing artists talk of their crafts. To me, a wonderful book is one that takes me on a journey into something I didn't know before." At Doubleday, she focused mostly on biographies and history. Jackie once told one of her authors, Jonathan Cott, that there is an old famous Egyptian prayer repeated by the scribes over centuries and centuries: "To speak of the Dead is to bring them back to life."

In 1986, when Jonathan Cott completed the first draft of his manuscript, she invited him to her office to study a collection of her private books on ancient Egyptian history, art and religion, including one of the enormous twenty-four volumes of the *Description de l'Egypte* commissioned by Napoleon. The book Jonathan Cott wrote, *The Search for Omm Sety*, is the story of a twentieth-century English-Egyptian priestess of Isis. Isis is the most famous Egyptian mother goddess to rule over the sky, land, seas, heavens and underworld. An Englishwomen named Dorothy Eady believed she was reincarnated as the Egyptian Isis priestess Omm Sety. Jackie informed Jonathan that in 1974, while taking a cruise on the Nile with Aristotle Onassis, they met Dorothy Eady/Omm Sety. She was living in a mud hut in the Upper Egyptian village of Abydos until her death in 1981. Madame Desroches Noblecourt, the egyptologist who organized the first King Tutankhamen exhibit at the National Gallery on November 3rd, 1961, admired Jackie's early support of her efforts to preserve the Nubian temples. Noblecourt agreed to act as a tour guide to Jackie, Ari, Caroline and John and that's how Jackie met Dorothy Eady in 1974.

"I love how his mind works," Jackie said about Jonathan Cott and commissioned a second book titled *Isis and Osiris: Exploring the Goddess Myth* in 1993. The Egyptian Madonna love mythology of Isis and Osiris predates the Christian Mary and Joseph story by thousands of years. When Osiris is destroyed, and his limbs are scattered over Egypt, Isis sets off on a journey to make her husband's body and soul one with her again.

It is a fable about sacrifice and a true and perfect love. Jonathan Cott once said about Jackie, "Listening to my editor's knowledgeable ideas about ancient Egypt, I soon began to imagine that like Omm Sety, I, too, was entering the world of ancient Egypt, conversing with an Egyptian queen who was as beautiful as Nefertiti . . ."

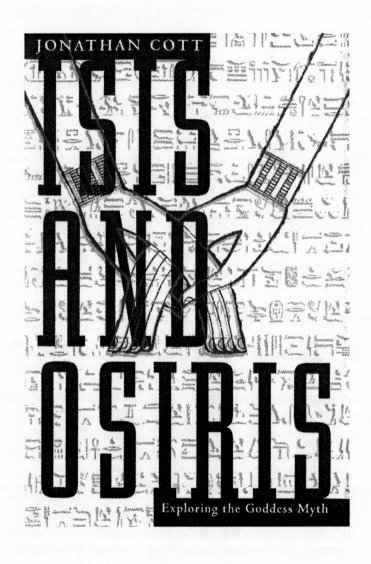

Upon hearing the details of Jonathan Cott's allusion to Nefertiti, Jackie's step-brother Yusha Auchincloss, added to the reference, "I always thought Jackie was more of a Catherine the Great." The Russian empress once remarked in 1759: 'If I may venture to be frank, I would say about myself, that I was every inch a gentleman.'"

When Naguib Mahfouz, author of *The Cairo Trilogy: Palace Walk, Palace of Desire* and *Sugar Street*, won the Nobel Prize for Literature, Jackie read *The Cairo Trilogy* in French and persuaded Doubleday to publish the American edition. Jackie notes, "They are lovely, these were designed by Alex Gottfryd, the late Doubleday art director. See how each cover has an antique photograph from a different era, reflecting the book's content." Her penetrating eye touched every aspect of the book's production quality, so each book has a unique look and feel. "I never got to meet Mahfouz, he doesn't travel, but we corresponded."

Robert Lyons, a photographer, learned through friends in Cairo that Naguib Mahfouz woke early each morning and walked to the Ali Baba Cafe to read dozens of international newspapers and savor his Turkish coffee. He followed his friend's advice, and discovered the Egyptian novelist sitting alone, facing the view of the city street down below. "Ahalan wasahlan," offered Mahfouz, sparked a cafe rendez-vous friendship fueled by a mutual passion for the drama of Egypt buttressed by an immense architectural mythology. Years later, a shared philosophical adventure was chronicled in *Egyptian Time*. Robert Lyons photographed an Egypt lost between two worlds: broken pedestals lay in an open field in Thebes, Pompey's Pillar in Alexandria, a Memphis landscape dotted with palm trees and desolate little homes, a turquoise blue Cairo interior on Gumhuriya Street, tired men waiting until a camel market opens in Imbaba and a humble entry to the Mosque of Al-Mordani. These images tell a story of a debilitating struggle with poverty, while a nation looks for its future.

Jackie commissioned Mahfouz to write a lyrical short story for the large volume of photography in *Egyptian Time*: "In the still of the night, the call to dawn prayers is heard, and the heart pounds at the approach of morning and playtime. On the pillow lies the figure of a great traveler, made of painted tin, he asks him if he has voyage to fairyland and seen wonders. There is so much to love; peddlers, boyscouts, circus parades, mobs of noisy boys, country relatives, and their tales of bogeymen, ghosts, and highwaymen, but every story has a happy ending."

PHOTOGRAPHY ADVENTURES

Jackie's fascination with several photographers inspired lavish visual exposes on the art of Eugene Atget, Peter Beard, Marc Riboud, Deborah Turbeville, Robert Lyons, William Eggleston and Toni Frissell. Karl Katz, the consulting producer for the film *Jackie: Behind the Myth,* suggested interviews with founding members of Magnum, Cornell Capa and the French photographer Marc Riboud. Karl described how they, Jacqueline Onassis, Karl Katz and Marc Riboud, all founding board members of the International Center for Photography (ICP), supported the revered photographer Cornell Capa's dream to establish a photography museum on Fifth Avenue.

Karl Katz in the Spring of 1997 detailed his history with Onassis and photographers Cornell Capa and Marc Riboud to establish the International Center for Photography. To honor this special occasion, Jackie wrote an article for the January 1975 issue of *The New Yorker* titled "Being Present" about Karl and Cornell and the opening of ICP on Fifth Avenue. Jackie interviews Karl, writing down his observations: "Here this says it better than I can. It's from Cornell's introduction in his book *The Concerned Photographer.* He pointed to the lines, 'Lewis W. Hine, an early humanitarian-with-a-camera may have stated it best: There were two things I wanted to do. I wanted to show the things that had to be corrected. I wanted to show the things that had to be appreciated.'"

In a discussion at ICP with Marc Riboud, he described his trip to China with Jackie. "She joined me while I was photographing at the University of Beijing. She took notes, I took pictures. On that day, I mentioned to her my passion for a mist-enshrouded mountain that for centuries inspired Chinese painters." Marc Riboud explained that the peaks of the mountain reach beyond the clouds so this region of Chinese geography is named Capital of Heaven. In one of his photographs, he pointed to the steps that disappear into the clouds, "those mountains were a place of tragic ritual for lovers to escape into 'heaven' from forbidden marriages, forsaken love or from the pain of losing a true love." Marc Riboud told Jackie that lovers climbed the mountains to commit suicide. Then he said, "And five years later she made a book possible with this very title."

One of the first ICP exhibitions, included Peter Beard's photography of Africa. A huge retrospective exhibition at his downtown gallery mirrors that first exhibition in 1975. The most obvious change is that thirty years later, the images are now enormous, no longer pictures, they are collage murals of African wildlife draping the walls of The Time Is Always Now. From floor to ceiling, Beard's diary-photographs of his life in Africa, transport you on a visual safari.

Peter Beard's photography book *Longing For Darkness* about Baroness Karen Dinesen Blixen, was inspired by her African odyssey. After he read her novel *Out of Africa*, his life was given a new direction. In 1937, Baroness Karen Dinesen Blixen observed ravaging colonialism in her journey-novel *Out of Africa*: "It is more than their land that you take away from the people . . . it is their past as well, their roots and their identity . . ." Baroness Blixen's identity was submerged into the adventurer-writer Isak Dinesen after she departed for Kenya to run a coffee plantation with her husband. In *The Human Condition*, Isak Dinesen muses, "All sorrows can be borne if you put them into a story or tell a story about them."

Peter fondly recalls, "Jackie loved *Longing For Darkness* and wrote an essay for Kamante Gatura, Blixen's Kikuyu cook and man-servant, who was a central figure in *Out of Africa*. I illustrated Kamante's diary who was devoted to Karen. Later on I traveled with John and Caroline on a safari."

The book accompanied an exhibition to celebrate the opening of the International Center for Photography. Jackie's introduction addresses the poetry in African life, "One of my favorite passages in *Out of Africa* is when Isak Dinesen asks, 'If I know a song of Africa, of the giraffe and the African new moon lying on her back, . . . does Africa know a song of me . . . would the eagles of the Ngong Hills look out for me?" She writes: "This book is the echo she longed for. Yes, Africa does have a song for her. It is Peter Beard and Kamante who have made it for her. Kamante's drawings and Peter Beard's photographs share a purity, of a wild animal looking at the camera with free and vulnerable eyes." This photo-graphic journey is the touchstone for Beard's early passions. His dreams belong with Isak Dinesen's in Africa, where Beard's life story in Kenya flourished at his camp, Hog Ranch.

Kamante's journal observations reveal Blixen's impression on the native people, "Mrs. Karen had to tell her people not to have quarrels, and if anybody quarreled she got very angry . . . God bring peace and compromise to her shamba. She never wanted any tribalism. To the Mkamba, Meru, Masai, Somali, or Kikuyu, 'I want you to be good people of God.' We all agreed with her."

At Doubleday, Jackie edited illustrated volumes to accom-pany exhibitions at The Metropolitan Museum of Art. *A Sec-ond Paradise: Indian Courtly Life, 1590-1947* accompanied an Indian costume exhibition at The Costume Institute in 1985. Both *A Second Paradise* and *The Garden of Life* by Naveen Patnaik are illustrated with paintings by Bannu, a master artist in the Jaipur School of Miniature Paintings. *The Garden of Life* is il-lustrated with artists' miniature paintings from significant re-gions in India depicting life in tender shades of vibrant color, etched in an exquisitely detailed realism. Toni Frissell's long overdue photography book is dedicated to Jackie, Eudora Welty wrote an essay describing William Eggleston's photographs in *The Democratic Forest*. In addition to *Atget's Gardens*, she commissioned Antony Beever and Artemis Cooper's *Paris After the Liberation, 1944 to 1949*.

In Deborah Turbeville's photography volume *Unseen Versailles* Jackie prevails, "Another photography book of Versailles? Are not the coffee tables groaning already? But wait!" Then she answers her own question, "No one has imposed her particular vision of this monument known to all. Her lens records the splendor of boiserie and stone and the mystery of unseen corners of private apartments . . . backstairs . . . backstage . . . she takes us through a labyrinth peopled by the ghosts of her imagination. It is Watteau, it is Hubert Robert, it is Dali, it is Edgar Allen Poe . . ." Versailles, a celestial palace of beauty celebrating architecture, painters, ballet and operatic music, was Jackie's inspiration for her White House state dinners.

In amusing detail Deborah Turbeville told the story of creating her book, after meeting Jackie through her long time fashion mentor Diana Vreeland. Deborah's voice the day she spoke about her 'project with Mrs. Onassis' started off calmly, "Well, Mrs. Vreeland did a book called *Allure* with Jacqueline. What she thought was either amusing or strange or bizarre or extraordinarily beautiful, and her favorite choices of fashion photography. From the most insignificant thing to Maria Callas, some incredible paparazzi pictures and all kinds of amazing things. Diana Vreeland heard about me from Andy Warhol's studio The Factory and other avant garde projects. She felt like there was a new, edgy, photographer working in the fashion world at that moment. And Mrs. Vreeland wanted to see my photographs. And when she did, she wanted to publish them. So Jackie got to see my work and then I was invited to a lunch with Mrs. Vreeland."

Deborah Turbeville's photographs are fantasy allegories that capture lost and forgotten worlds. When she photographs an eighteenth century ballroom, she recreates a scene of passion with relics and models dressed in period, so that the room is filled with the emotion of another era. Not only is she a great photographer, but she became a real friend of Jackie's.

Deborah's voice gathered a lively beat as she ventured into her story, "About a year or two later, I got a strange phone call. This familiar voice said, 'This is Jacqueline Onassis. I'm looking for Deborah Turbeville. If you know where she is, I'd love to talk to her about doing a book project with me.' I never met her so it was quite an amazing, a really amazing thing for me. I called her back and she said, 'I just wanted to pass it by you.'

Jackie described the idea of the book to Deborah, "I discovered there are some very special, unknown rooms at Versailles. I was taken on a tour of these rooms and I can't think of anyone more appropriate to photograph the back rooms of Versailles than you, would you do it?"

Deborah sounded as if she was talking over the idea with her editor. "I don't know, it's hard to know at this point what it would mean in my life. I'd like to think about it. I think I could do it." Deborah and Jacqueline soon agreed on the project and in several meetings discussed the concept for the book. Together they traveled to tour the secret back-rooms at Versailles. She recounted in whimsical detail the entire journey. When she saw the rooms, she was totally disillusioned and very upset. She left Versailles in a quandary, feeling that the idea didn't warrant a book.

Deborah did not confide her deepest fears to Jackie. "It didn't interest me, it didn't excite me. And what do you do when someone wants a kind of incredible miracle from you, for you to bring off an idea of theirs and you don't feel it's there? I say that because Versailles had been manicured so heavily with the system of curating. It wasn't me. It wasn't my texture and my feeling. And so I felt that I couldn't do it. And I went through some very bad moments about this. I didn't speak to Jacqueline about it. And then finally I was working with a very interesting woman who was going to help me style the book and knew my work. And we both were discouraged after the tour. I finally decided to talk to Jacqueline. We wanted to put costumes on a few models and create a kind of fantasy. And so Jacqueline and I went to Versailles to meet the curator."

On the way to Versailles, Jackie said to Deborah, "Don't bring it up. It's already difficult enough Deborah without getting into asking for permission to bring costumes and people and animals in here. You know he's going to think it's a Fellini film. That's not the mentality of these people. You know they're curators."

Deborah looked into the air of her study as if she saw her editor, and with a chuckle that turned into half laughing, half speaking, she said, "Well you know, Mrs. Onassis, I feel very strongly . . . and she said, 'Don't bring it up.' So we have this amazing meeting with this little bureaucrat." Deborah was really laughing now. "But he was utterly charmed and staggered by her, having her in his office. And he would have said yes if she'd told him to jump out of the window."

Deborah was lost in her great story, "Later on, I'm sure when he mulled the whole thing over, he thought what have I said I'd let her do?" Deborah said, "Jacqueline, you still didn't ask him about these models." Jackie warned her, "We'll bring it up slowly. You don't know how to do this. There is a certain protocol."

Deborah was ignited by the idea of using models in costumes. "Jacqueline left and I thought I'm going to start working with my costume lady. I'm going to find those strange people and make my Fellini film at Versailles. And I saw Versailles as an old crone, who'd had an unfortunate face lift and who would be more beautiful withered without it. So that's the Versailles that I went about trying to present to my editor."

Then, Deborah reminded Jackie about the costumes and models. Jackie said, "Oh all right, I'll call him." So she called Deborah back and said, "All right, a few people that's all. And you know, he'll have to see these pictures before they're published."

In the dark winter month of January, Deborah left for Versailles. In retrospect, she recalls, "The light was low and when you looked through the mirrors, the mirrors were reflecting all the rooms. In strange, murky ways, it all became exactly what I wanted."

Deborah marched on, "It was the most amazing thing. It was a three ring circus with all the people we found and the costumes. We even brought in trained monkeys, we did everything we thought we could get away with. At ten o'clock at night, there would be nothing but candelabra. A big candelabra and all of us, with the girls in the costumes. Farthingales mind you, those things that go out to here. And the monkeys and everything would parade down the staircase. We really felt like it was what it could have been like in the old days. We really got the essence of the atmosphere. We were also aware that no one really did this very often. We were, you know, rarefied people to have been allowed to do it."

To bring the ghosts of Versailles back to life was the photographer's dream. She recalled how Jackie admired Madame de Pompadour. Deborah reminiscences, "I think in a way, Jacqueline felt that she was a kind of modern Madame de Pompadour. Because she was such a patron of the arts. She was a very romantic figure. Jacqueline said to me, 'Oh dear, but you have to read this Nancy Mitford book.'"

"Surely a King who loves pleasure is less dangerous than one who loves glory!" The English wit, novelist and biographer, Nancy Mitford (1904–1973) observes in her essay *In Defense of Louis XV*. Nancy Mitford also wrote a wonderful biography of Madame de Pompadour. Jackie told Deborah, "It's a very moving, her book." Deborah observes, "The whole fairytale quality of Louis XV's Versailles was what captivated both of us. It was like a fairytale at one point when Louis XV reigned particularly. And then the whole tragedy of the kingdom and the end of it."

Both Jackie and Deborah admired Madame de Pompadour, a brilliant mistress of Louis XV's, who introduced a sublime whimsy to the court through her deep love and knowledge of the arts and culture. In 1765 the new maitresse declaree moved into Versailles. Her recent title of marquis did not distinguish her from other court aristocratic ladies, as Madame de Pompadour was born a Poisson, from a middle-class background. Louis Auchincloss writes, "It was predicted that her reign would be a brief one, and there were many at court who did not bother to cultivate her favor." The Marquis de Pompadour, a long-time favorite of Louis XV, proved them all wrong. "Almost twenty years later, her influence of the king was still transcendent." After the king tired of her physical beauty, she encourage the prostitutes of his beloved brothel to attend to his needs. Until her death, she ruled in his orbit, cultivating poets, painters and dancers for the king's entertainment, thus hanging on to his heart and his mind. In her gardens, she erected a statue *Friendship*, and lovingly place her hand over his heart and "with a charming smile, tinged with the appearance of a faint regret, a mild melancholy, she would cry, There is all that I care about."

At Versailles, Deborah's photography sessions were causing an uproar. "Jacqueline had been forceful. But still, every night there were two little Corsican twin brothers, the Albertini brothers. They were very sweet and they would come with us during the day. And at night they would just say sorry, Monsieur Lamonde has to see these Polaroids. And so the next day he would say this can't be published."

Deborah described the working class protocol, "And it's a whole family there of workers who work on that place. The Albertini brothers said we do not wish to interfere with an artist when she's working. So therefore we are resigning this part of our job. And then they put a hunchback in. He came every day and asked for the Polaroids. This went on and on."

Monsieur Lamonde was so angry, he finally called Jackie and said, "I won't allow this anymore because I have heard that she is Lady Hamilton." Jackie called Deborah and repeated the conversation, " . . . And that Lady Hamilton took pornographic pictures and he couldn't allow it at Versailles."

Deborah said to Jacqueline, "What do you mean?"

Jackie amusingly replies, "You know Deborah, he thinks that you are David Hamilton who does all of those soft porn pictures. He doesn't know the difference."

Deborah gasped, "You know Jacqueline, my pictures are never like that.

Jackie laughed, "Don't even talk to me about it. It's not even to be discussed. I calmed him down so go ahead and finish. But hurry."

Deborah was like a child now caught in some mischief, "So then, there was one more episode in the Napoleonic Wing. The Napoleonic Wing had been bombed and never restored. And they hadn't found the money to repair it yet. It was a kind of Hubert Robert painting in itself. The statues' heads had rolled on to the floor. And there were things falling and broken pedestals. Pediments and all this kind of stuff. And I thought this is just a dream. I said let me go get my make-up and hair man Anthony. I think we can do something extraordinary. Anthony said don't even talk to me. I'm not even going to tell you what I'm going to do. Well you know people who have worked in the fashion world. And he started doing this bald head wrapping that you do before you put the wig on. And you leave no hair showing. The petticoat with the bando was (flaired) out to here. And we obviously were going to have the girls cascading or falling down the staircase. It took four hours, he got up at four in the morning to evolve this thing. And he was just putting the finishing touches on, so I sent my assistant over to do Polaroids for Monsieur Lamonde. And she ran back and said there are guards outside. All the shutters are down. And I've been told to tell you to call Monsieur Lamonde immediately."

Deborah said, "You know, I'm not in the mood to call him. I'm ready to work here. What does he think he's doing? He's interfering with my picture."

The entrance to the Napoleonic Wing had been blockaded with wheelbarrows and guards. The assistant said, "Deborah you are not getting in there if you don't make a call."

Deborah was determined, "So I called. And he said, 'Madame, I do not want you in that place. That is off limits. You were not given permission. Every day you have to send a typed list with your request of places and it is approved or not approved. That place was not approved. "

Deborah said, "But Monsieur Lamonde, I don't think you understand."

The palace curator's tolerance evaporated with his flat refusal, "I understand very well."

Deborah said, "This is a very poetic picture. "

He burst out, "I don't care how poetic it is."

Monsieur Lamonde told Deborah, "I am sure that it is a very poetic picture. But not in my museum."

That was the end of the conversation. Deborah didn't get into the Napoleonic Wing. Jackie called Deborah, "We're running out of time. Doubleday won't publish this book if you don't get this back to me."

The real problem was not one that revolved around a deadline. The photographer was in a great hailstorm of anxiety trying to understand what went wrong with her pictures. She explained, "I tried to keep the color like my own color. I couldn't pull it off because the electrical outlets were so low that we couldn't use the kind of lights I would use. It would balance the daylight and make the light very soft and gauzy. So we had to use a kind of strobe flash. But a very soft powered one that was guaranteed to give me the same effect. And frankly it didn't work. And when I got the color back, I hated most of the color. I was ready to go down to the Seine and throw it in. I salvaged what I could of it. And converted most of it to black and white. And then we did two or three processes to tint it a little. I didn't want the color, I just wanted something faded."

Jackie was in New York trying to pull the magic out of her artist. So Deborah submerged herself on an island off the coast of France where she had rented a cottage and worked on the layouts. A month went by and when she called her editor, Jackie said, "This is the eleventh hour."

In New York, Deborah reluctantly showed the Doubleday art director the photographs in both a lush colorful version and her preferred faded blue-gray tinted pictures. Deborah sighed, then in a low voice said, "And I kind of held my breath." Her voice lit up, "But, they loved the faded version."

Deborah's excited editor reveals her devotion, "Well now what we have to do is find you the ideal book designer to help you pull this together. That's the most important thing we have to do."

Jackie was guiding the vision of Turbeville, while at the same time thinking of ways to make the book enlightening. To describe the social history of the photographs, Jackie consulted her long time friend Louis Auchincloss. He agreed to write a description of the Versailles apartments, and the extravagant private affairs of the aristocrats. "A lady of the bed-chamber of Marie-Antoinette states in the preface of her memoirs: 'We all love to delve into the private lives of the princes.'"

Jackie's art director found Michael Flanagan who according to Turbeville, "was the perfect, perfect, perfect designer for the book," and that's how she got her book finished. Deborah adds, "And it was because Jacqueline from beginning to end, was there for me as an editor. You very rarely get so much attention. Because these are special little books. And you don't usually get that much attention. You're usually on your own or working with someone who is a little bit less sympathetic to your vision." On the reported claims that Jackie was a part-time editor, Deborah Turbeville angrily snapped, "I mean it just makes me so mad sometimes when I realize that people have such a shallow idea of not just Jacqueline, but other people in the arts too. I have to remind them, Jacqueline was the best editor I ever had."

HAMMERSMITH FARM AND TSAR NICHOLAS

One of Jackie's authors, Edvard Radzinsky, a scholar in 20th century Russian history authored biographies of *Tsar Nicholas II*, then *Stalin*. The discovery that she edited nearly ten books on Russian culture and history reveals a life long passion for Russia's struggle for peace. Hugh D. 'Yusha' Auchincloss, her half-Russian stepbrother, lives in Newport on Hammersmith Farm. In several discussions during the winter of 2000, he reveals his thoughts on Radzinsky, Nikita Khrushchev, the cultural legacy of Russia, and his Russian genealogy. His observations on Jackie's early interest in the fall of the Romanov empire and the Lenin/Stalin regime's political strategies to suppress Russian culture reveals Jackie's compassion for artists after the Russian Revolution.

In Newport, one January winter evening, Yusha described the story of his White Russian mother, and Jackie's feelings for her plight. Yusha's mother, Maya Charapovitsky, was the daughter a Tsarist naval officer, a White Russian. She served as a nurse's aid in World War I. Then after the assassination of the Romanov dynasty, she fled to the United States. She fell in love with Hugh D. Auchincloss, Yusha's father, then married him. He said, "Oh Jackie knew all about my mother, and admired her for surviving!"

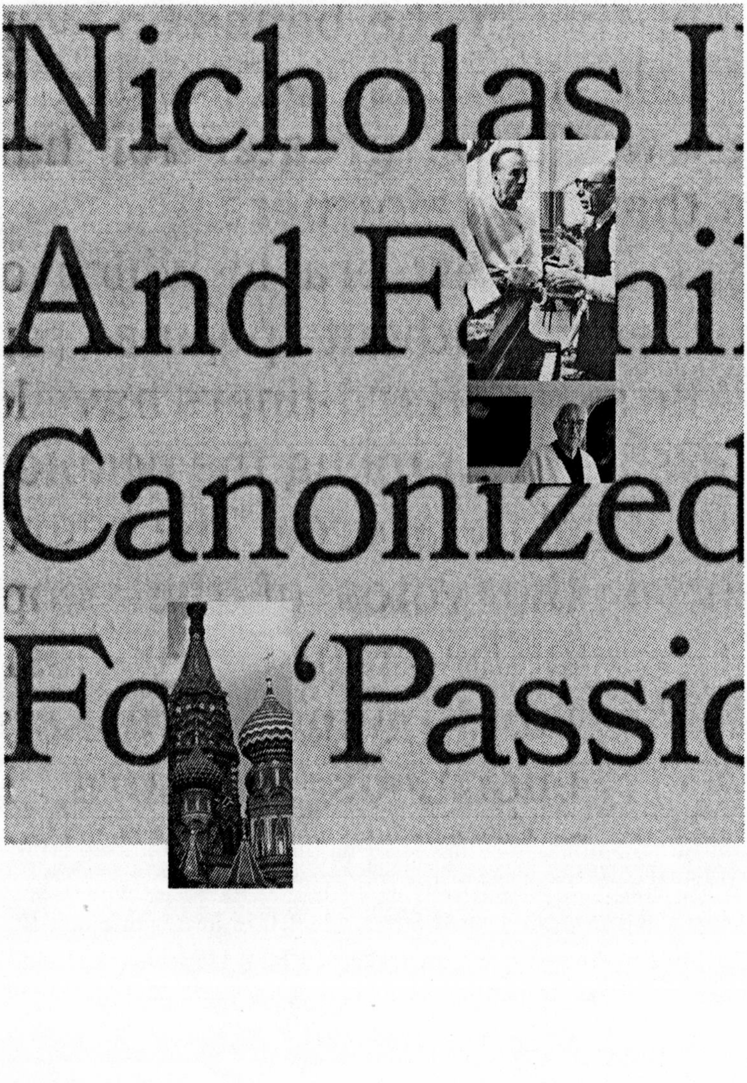

The long history of Russian ballet before the fall of the Romanov empire may be traced to 1673 when a ballet based on the theme of *Orpheus* was presented to the court of Tsar Aleksei Mikhailovich. The performance marked the beginning of the imperial patronage of Russian theater, dance and ballet, a foundation that enabled the ballet to survive in Russia long after its viability as an art form in Western Europe had ceased. The sovereign Peter I actually taught others to dance and it was well-known that the tsar could perform cabrioles that would impress any European ballet master. The arrival of French ballet masters in 1738 established the tradition of a national ballet school in St. Petersburg. In 1756, Catherine II, memorialized as Catherine the Great, created a state theater monopoly that guaranteed the future of Russian ballet. She founded the Imperial theater school, the Imperial theater system and ordered the construction of St. Petersburg Bolshoi Theater in 1773. The cultural legacy Catherine the Great created includes The Hermitage Museum which miraculously survived the purging of the arts during the Lenin-Stalin regime. Not long after Charles-Louis Didelot and Arthur Saint-Leon, important French ballet masters teaching in St. Petersburg, emerged the great Russian masters Marius Petipa (1818-1910). Sergei Diaghilev's Ballet Russes and Balanchine are proteges of Petipa's tradition.

Yusha discussed Tsar Nicholas, the slaying of the White Russians when Lenin came to power, the thirty million innocent Russians slaughtered by Stalin and Jackie's fascination with Russian history and culture. She studied the Diaghilev Ballet as a young girl. While first lady, George Balanchine inspired her, and she supported all the Russian ballerinas in the New York City Ballet. The Bolshoi Ballet performed in Washington on November 13, 1962, right after the Cuban Missile Crisis, and Jackie insisted on attending. Jackie religiously studied the Russian ballet as if it was an ancient oracle expressing the Russian spirit in a transcendental ritual of dance.

In the late 1950's in New York City, Jacqueline Kennedy often attended Balanchine's ballet dress rehearsals and she knew the origins and history of the Russian ballerinas. In the summer of 1924, Balanchine fled Lenin's newly formed Soviet Union with three dancers Tamara Geva, Alexandra Danilova and Nicholas Efimov on a tour of Western Europe. At the same time, Igor Stravinsky, who trained at the Mariinsky Theatre in St. Petersburg, was Sergei Diaghilev's 'composer in residence' for his Ballets Russes company in Paris. That company created *The Firebird* performance in 1910. Stravinsky stayed in Paris and spent much of his future time continuing his collaborations with Diaghilev in *Petrushka* (1911) and *The Rite of Spring* (1913). In 1924, Balanchine and the dancers were invited by impresario Sergei Diaghilev to audition for his Ballets Russes and were accepted into the company. Diaghilev had his eye on Balanchine as a choreographer. After watching him stage a new version of the company's Stravinsky ballet, *Le Chant de Rossignol*, Diaghilev appointed him as ballet master.

In 1933, Sergei Diaghilev died, and Europe appeared closed to Balanchine because all the big jobs were awarded to natives of each country. Lincoln Kirstein, a poet, art historian and ballet advocate, invited Balanchine to come to America knowing that his rigorous training had prepared Balanchine for a new adventure in the culturally unsophisticated country. The son of a composer, Balanchine, early in life, gained a knowledge of music that far exceeds most of his fellow choreographers. He began studying the piano at the age of five. Following his graduation in 1921 from the Imperial Ballet School in St. Petersburg, he enrolled in the Conservatory of Music. He studied piano and musical theory, including composition, harmony and counterpoint, for three years. Such extensive musical training made it possible for Balanchine as a choreographer to communicate with a composer of such stature as Igor Stravinsky. The training also gave Balanchine the ability to reduce orchestral scores on the piano, an invaluable aid in translating music into dance.

In 1941, Balanchine and Kirstein assembled the American Ballet Caravan, sponsored by Nelson Rockefeller, which toured

South America with such new Balanchine creations as *Concerto Barocco*. In 1946, Balanchine and Kirstein collaborated again to form Ballet Society, a company which introduced New York subscription-only audiences over the next two years to such new Balanchine works as Stravinsky's *Renard* in 1947 and *Orpheus* in 1948. Morton Baum, chairman of the City Center finance committee, saw Ballet Society during one of its subscription programs at City Center. Baum was so highly impressed that he invited the company to join the City Center municipal complex which at the time the New York City Drama Company and the New York City Opera were a part, as the "New York City Ballet." Balanchine's talents at last had found a permanent home. On October 11, 1948, the New York City Ballet was conceived, dancing a program consisting of *Concerto Barocco, Orpheus and Symphony in C.*

A young Jacqueline Bouvier was aware of impresario Sergei Diaghilev links to choreographer George Balanchine and the legendary Ballets Russes in Paris. As a young women, she once said that she loved reading 'anything about the ballet'. When she was twenty-one, in her 1951 first place Vogue Prix de Paris exposition, she wished she had known Diaghilev and discusses "a common theory on the interrelation of the arts".

Her bemused Bouvier observations continue; "Sergei Diaghilev dealt not with the interaction of the senses but with an interaction of the arts, an interaction of the cultures of East and West. Though not an artist himself, he possessed what is rarer than artistic genius in any one field; the sensitivity to take the best of each man and incorporate it into a masterpiece all the more precious because it lives only in the minds of those who have seen it and disintegrates as soon as he is gone."

The new first lady supported artists who performed and taught advanced training of music and ballet to advise her plans to elevate the national awareness of culture. For many years, her old friend George Balanchine, like a missionary, conducted free seminars for ballet teachers in America and organized free ballets for children.

When Balanchine agreed to a White House visit, he advised her how to broaden support for the ballet, music and dance. Balanchine, charmed by her graciousness, later told a television journalist that, "I would only want to be president if I could have Jacqueline Kennedy as my first lady, and then, with her help, do what should be done to bring beauty into people's lives." After her White House years, Jackie's long admiration for the Diaghilev ballet inspired the Kennedy Center to honor George Balanchine, Igor Stravinsky, Tamara Geva and Alexandra Danilova.

In 1975, when Jackie became a book editor at Viking Press, the first books she commissioned *In The Russian Style* in 1976 and *The Firebird and Other Russian Fairy Tales* with Boris Zvorykin in 1978 were illustrated according to her editorial style and advice. She longed to capture her compassion for the forgotten cultures of the extraordinary period during the Romanov regimes. *In The Russian Style* was designed to catalog Diana Vreeland's costume exhibition at The Metropolitan Museum of Art. Old friends from before Jackie's White House years, Diana Vreeland and Jackie traveled to Moscow and St. Petersburg to select the costumes and research the photographs for the book *In The Russian Style*.

At Doubleday, she commissioned dance critic, Francis Mason, to write a biography of Balanchine, *I Remember Balanchine*, and continued to explore the Russian legacy with the following books: Vasily Peskov wrote *Lost in the Taige: One Family's Fifty-Year Struggle for Survival and Religious Freedom in the Siberian Wilderness*, Rudolph Nureyev wrote the introduction to a book of fairytales by Aleksandr Pushkin *The Golden Cockerel and Other Fairy Tales* with illustrations by Boris Zvorykin. Daniel Boorstin edited the Marquis de Custine's memoir titled *Empire of the Tsar*.

In the early nineties, Jackie was introduced to the Russian history scholar Edvard Radzinsky. He could barely speak English the first time he met his editor, 'Mrs. Onassis' in 1991. Jackie worked with the author on the historical account of Tsar Nicholas, and started to edit his next book *Stalin*, but she died before its publication. When he spoke of her death, he said, "And she died by first lady of century. She was incredible noble woman. That, I know. And she had faith of first lady. It was maybe main in her character. And her faith and her life was on her face. When I saw her, I immediately understood that she was queen. I am play-wright and I know it's impossible to play queen."

Radzinsky began working with Jackie right around the time Oliver Stone's film *JFK* was in the theaters. He felt that President Kennedy's assassination was such a great shock to her, that unless she offered to discuss the topic, he could never say anything about it. Intuition gave him the answer for her interest in his book. "And when my literary agent told me that she was interested in my book, I understood im-mediately. I understood because assassination of Kennedy was one of the top mysteries of this century. And assassination of the Tsar's fam-ily continued to be top mystery of the century too."

Rather Radzinsky offered religious parallels found in the *Bible* that illustrates how human behavior and emotions have in ancient history sometimes explained modern men's actions and reactions to powerful personalities in history and world events. "I avoid the mystery of assassination. I avoid these words. I tried to have con-versation with her only about religious moments. You see, a reli-gious moment was most important to me in my book, more like words in the *Bible*."

After John F. Kennedy's assassination, Jackie in an interview to Theodore White described her husband's presidency as Camelot and she told the journalist, "History . . . it's what those bitter old men write." Radzinsky observes, "She understood my book by feelings. It's much more truthful."

Radzinsky, a man of the theater and an historian grasped what Jackie may have felt many historians fail to reveal, that human emotions, and not just the critical judgment of the facts and the exterior motivations, are equally important. "And she understood my main idea. She understood that for me it's my mission. I did not write the book about terrible Bolsheviks who execute that family. No. I wrote a book about forgiveness. About people who were able to forgive before their death. And their legacy for my country was their forgiveness." The scholar and the former first lady connected on a deeper level, perhaps in a way that gave her a better understanding of her own experience.

On October 17, 1905, Tsar Nicholas Romanov observed a recurring theme in Russian history, "Lord save Russia and bring her peace." There were political and historical themes that could be addressed in Radzinsky's book that would further explain the American fear of Communism and the Cold War. Radzinsky recalls, "It's main thought for Russia. We have today the same collapse of former empire. And we have today the same question what to do. And she understood that the main question for Russia was what to do. It was main idea of my book too."

When he was granted permission into the Russian archives, Radzinsky discovered the emotional equivalent of the ark of the lost covenant. When the Central Russian Archives were briefly opened, he sorted through the secret files of the All-Russian Executive Committee, once the highest power in revolutionary Russia. He discovered one file dated 1918-1919, a year after the executions of the Tsar and his family. Radzinsky writes that it was "The Apocalypse as recorded by a witness." The whole horrible night of July 16th to 17th, 1918 was dispassionately recorded, even the secret locations of the Tsar and his family members' graves.

On July 16, Alexei Romanov wrote in his diary that his sister Tatiana read in the Bible from the book of the prophet Obadiah: "And their king shall go into captivity, and he and his princes together, saith the Lord. The Lord God hath sworn by his holiness, that, lo, the days shall come upon you, that he will take you away with hooks . . ."

"Behold, the days come, saith the Lord God, that I will send a famine in the land; not a famine of bread, nor a thirst for water, but of hearing the words of the Lord." The Romanov family was executed on July 17, 1918 by an edict sent from Moscow. The biblical quote ends, "And they shall wander from sea to sea, and from the north even to the east; they shall run to and fro to see the word of the Lord, and shall not find it . . ."

STALIN

THE FIRST IN-DEPTH

BIOGRAPHY BASED ON

EXPLOSIVE NEW

DOCUMENTS FROM

RUSSIA'S SECRET ARCHIVES

EDVARD RADZINSKY

AUTHOR OF *THE LAST TSAR*

The Last Tsar capitulated the idea to get Radzinsky back into
the Russian archives to write a history of Stalin. Jackie told
Radzinsky, "Hurry. Hurry, try to do it much more quickly."
Radzinsky continues, "She knows that our archives were opened.
It was short time. Today they are not so open believe me. It was
very short time. And it was ocean of new documents. Ocean. It's
impossible to leave because every day new documents appeared."

Radzinsky explained to Jackie how Stalin, a trained priest,
twisted his motivations in his own mind to believe that his leadership was motivated by an inner goodness: "And I told her that it
would not be political portrait. It would be psychological portrait.
I told her small episode from Stalin's life after he became our leader.
Magnificent, incredible leader. He went to see his mother. Stalin
had a religious education, and once studied to be a priest. Instead
he became a revolutionary. His mother, a very religious woman,
asked him Soso—it's Stalin name for her, like small Joseph. Soso
who are you today? It was incredible question. And he answered
her I'm like tsar, you remember tsar? His mother said, 'I remember, but much better you should be a priest.' And she understood
how the devil changed his soul. It would be the book about the
man who refuse to be with Christ. Stalin created new, incredible
Babylon, but not like Nicholas. No."

On November 30th, 1943 Stalin celebrated his sixty-sixth
birthday with Winston Churchill and Averell Harriman, who was
President Roosevelt's personal emissary to both Churchill and
Stalin. During the course of the dinner and war strategy discussions, Stalin suggested shooting 50,000 German officers and tech-
nicians as soon as the war was over. A stunned Churchill replied:
"The British Parliament and public will never tolerate mass executions . . . I would rather be taken out into the garden here and
now and be shot myself than sully my own and my country's
honor by such infamy." Hitler's war crimes and killing of innocent
civilians were tripled by Stalin who proved to be the most vicious
to his own friends.

Radzinsky and Jackie discussed how Stalin killed his supporters, artists, writers and his friends. Yet, in his library, he was surrounded by their books, admiring the people who he murdered. Radzinsky writes: "All the arts were systematically savaged: literature, the theater, the cinema. Soon it was music's turn. The West's favorites, Prokofiev and Shostakovich, were the two composers most lambasted in a Central Committee edict of February 1947. As soon as the edict was published, Prokofiev wrote a penitential letter. His son observes that his father, 'suffered from exhausting headaches and chronic hypertomia. He was a different man, he always looked sad and hopeless.'" Coincidentally, on the day of Stalin's death, March 5, 1953, Sergei Prokofiev died. While Stalin was buried like a hero, the composer died in anonymity.

Edvard Radzinsky told Jackie that he found the remains of Stalin's library. The enormity of Stalin's evil erupted into the comment: "And he continued to read Trotsky, Bukharin, all his victims. He continued to have conversations with them in his notes, by his marks, and his notes."

In that last meeting, Jackie said to him, "That's great. That image." Many months later, while attending to the successful publication of *The Last Tsar* in Poland, Radzinsky heard about her death. He remembers thinking, "For me she did not die. She went out of the room and very soon she came back."

SAVING THE TEMPLES: DENDUR AND GRAND CENTRAL

Jackie once mused, "Great civilizations of the past recognized that their citizens had aesthetic needs, that great architecture gave nobility to their daily lives. They built fine buildings, spacious parks, beautiful markets. Their places of assembly, of worship, of ceremony, of arrival and departure were not merely functional but spoke to the dignity of man."

Yusha Auchincloss lectured why Newport's railroad barons' mansions, better known as 'cottages', are simply monuments to a European tradition of entertaining. As if temples to a royal perspective, the estates were designed to entertain emperors, maharajas, sultans, dukes, lords, marquis, princes, only closing the iron gates to a hungry dictator hoping to dine first class. Jacqueline Bouvier lived on Hammersmith Farm for ten years, and when she became First Lady, President Kennedy enjoyed playing golf at the Newport Country Club so much that the house was nicknamed The Little White House. The working farm is a metaphor for the American ideal of a pilgrim's way of life. Hammersmith Farm stands for something more than just faux monarchy, but a democratic way of thinking, and it is alone in this mission in Newport. Yusha once wrote that President Kennedy on his last visit to Hammersmith Farm to celebrate his tenth wedding anniversary, "thanked the Auchincloss family for making him feel 'at home' in the house he had admired as a young PT naval officer training out of Melville up the Narragansett Bay during World War II . . . on that cool, clear evening, while enjoying his daiquiri, the President reminisced about his Navy training days . . . and that he had always thought that the combined East-West view from his boat as he passed Hammersmith Farm was one of the loveliest sights in the whole country."

Yusha's library is stuffed with books on international politics and art from the thirties, forties on through to the late sixties. I found a copy of a rare first edition of JFK's *The Strategy of Peace* published in 1960. A speech describing the American failure to fund the Aswan Dam in Egypt in the 1950's tracked Yusha's early career as a specialist in Middle Eastern foreign policy to the United Nations. In the late fifties, he was a consultant to the World Bank when the loan to build the Aswan Dam was declined to Egypt. He points out that, "the floods were caused by the construction of the Aswan High Dam financed by the Communist Soviet Union." Then, with regret in his voice, he pointed to *The Strategy of Peace* and said, "I told Kennedy all about that. The Soviets came in, and the World Bank failed to make a commitment to that project. Eugene Black at the World Bank, and the British-American design was a much better plan for the Aswan Dam, but the Soviets prevailed over us. The Americans wanted to build twelve coffer dams to prevent those huge floods, rather than one large structure. It was a terrible mistake."

Andre Malraux wrote in his *Anti-memoirs*, "I hear the impatient drivers blowing their horns outside the Cairo Museum. . . . Here are photographs of work on the high dam—seventeen times taller than the pyramid of Cheops—which will give birth to a three hundred mile lake and the destruction of which by an atom bomb would annihilate Egypt. The yellow crane at Abu Simbel lifts up to the sky a bas-relief of prisoners, as if to dedicate it to the sun-god, Ra."

Yusha recalls, "I never met Andre Malraux, but he knew Jack and Jackie quite well." In 1998 discussions in Paris with the French archeologist/egyptologist Madame Christiane Desroches Noblecourt confirmed that Jackie was dedicated to preserving the Nubian monuments. "Jackie got involved with the efforts to save the temples from Egyptian floods," the egyptologist Madame Desroches Noblecourt specifically said, "with UNESCO and Andre Malraux's leadership, we organized the first American exhibition of antiquities from King Tutankhaman's tomb in 1961." Jackie, as First Lady, presided over the exhibition at the National Gallery in Washington D.C. Then President Kennedy passed a bill to send six million dollars in aid to prevent the colossal Egyptian temples at Abu Simbel from sinking into the Nile River due to the damaging floods.

The first King Tutankhamen exhibition at the National Gallery arrived on November 3, 1961. Egyptian President, Gamal Abdel Nasser honored her support with a 4,400 year old statue of an Egyptian man, and the gift was presented to Jackie at the exhibition. During her White House tenure, she was offered to select one of several temples as a memorial to the Kennedy administration. Jackie chose the Temple of Dendur, as she felt that the quality of the temple, and it's provenance was the most interesting. Dendur dates from Early Roman period, about 15 B.C. The temple was built by the Roman emperor Augustus and honors the goddess Isis and two deified sons of a local Nubian chieftain.

In December of 1964, Christiane Desroches Noblecourt authored an article in The UNESCO *Courier*, titled "Nubia's Sands Reveal Their Last Secrets." For the first time, the Nubian expedition united a worldwide effort, over fifty countries peaceful cooperation to preserve humanity's antiquity. It was she said, "an amazingly broad sweep of events encompassed by this vast breath-taking enterprise of united international cooperation and generosity." She describes major discoveries with astonishment: the unearthing of the fortress of Buhen buried until three years ago, objects in the region near a temple of Horus at Baki (Kuban) one of the most important temples of Egypt from the 5th B.C. century onward, the dismantling of the dromos known as the sacred avenue of sphinxes of Dakka, the location of a temple of almost gigantic proportions built during the reign of Amenophis III a prototype for the temples at Abu Simbel, and the recovery intact of the Coptic vase used in the consecration ceremonies which transformed the temples of Wadi es Sebua into a Christian church. That is a brief history of the major archaeological discoveries. Desroches Noblecourt summarizes the long expedition as: "Faith in an ideal can move mountains."

Jackie's history in regards to the Nubian expedition reveals that Yusha and Jackie shared a passion for Egypt's culture. "When the floods came, we were all very concerned about those temples." Yusha observes that, "Jackie was very proud of that statue of the Egyptian man. She had it on display in the front hall her Fifth Avenue apartment. Now it's at the Kennedy Library. Then the Temple of Dendur came later in 1965. In 1967, Brooke Astor provided funding for Tom Hoving at The Metropolitan Museum of Art to build a glass atrium to house the Temple of Dendur. There was a big fight over that because Jackie wanted it to go to Washington D.C. along the Potomac River as President Kennedy's memorial." Yusha observes, "Dendur is a memorial to both President Kennedy and Jackie."

After the death of President Kennedy, Jackie returned to New York City. Her fourteenth floor Fifth Avenue apartment provided privacy enabling her to entertain old friends without the intrusive Washington press waiting at her townhouse front door. Comforted by the memories of her childhood on Park Avenue, and afternoons in Central Park, she settled into her new home at 1040 Fifth Avenue built by her Irish grandfather James T. Lee. She soon bought a country home in Peapack, where she joined an exclusive equestrienne club in New Jersey. She continued her efforts to preserve architecture by joining the Municipal Art Society (MAS). Fred Papert, a friend of Robert Kennedy's was the president of MAS and the other board members, Kent Barwick, Ashton Hawkins and Karl Katz rallied around her missionary style efforts to save landmark buildings. The stinging loss of McKim Mead & White's majestic Pennsylvania Station was still a recent memory. Jackie joined an effort to save the Metropolitan Opera House in the '70's. That effort was not successful.

The Municipal Art Society was established on March 22nd, 1893, to halt 20th century developers leveling of New York City's architectural splendors. The losses, especially on Fifth Avenue above 42nd Street, are staggering in comparison to the new repetitious facades of look-alike skyscrapers built by architects/developers profiting from uninspired imitations of each other. Jackie once wrote, "As a young country, constantly reforming its image of itself, the United States tore down too much. We saw great buildings and cherished small scale neighborhoods disappear. The voice of preservationists was a lonely voice, powerless against mighty commercial interests." Other exceptional works of architecture lost to the profit motive include the German Winter Garden, a superb example of Egyptian architecture the Croton Reservoir, the Museum of Modern Art's first building and facade, and remarkable old mansions designed by Richard Morris Hunt for Mrs. John Jacobs Astor, Cornelius Vanderbuilt, the Apthorpe Mansion, Gothic villas, Greek palaces, and Romantic Classical architecture aimed at the Sublime in the tradition of Thomas Jefferson and Benjamin Latrobe's Greek temples.

"Jackie Onassis Fights for A Cause, " the headline ran in the

New York *Times*. "Jackie Onassis will save us," Philip Johnson, the
architect, saluted the former First Lady, who was among a troop of
well-known New Yorkers gathered for a press conference in the
Oyster Bar to save Grand Central Terminal. "Progress has been
made since that dismal time in 1963 when Philip Johnson, Alin
Saarinen, Peter Blake, Norval White, Eliz Parkison, Ulrich Franzen
and Peter Samton picketed alone in the snow to save Pennsylvania
Station. That battle was lost, and the loss is irreplaceable . . . then
the tide turned, the Landmarks Preservation Commission was
formed and Americans began to realize that it would never be
possible to build in the future as they had in the past, that old
buildings are a precious part of our heritage"

Phillip Johnson, a pillar of American Modernism and Mies
van der Rohe's protege, was well-versed on the irreversible conse-
quences of any threat to the old Beaux Art monument, Grand
Central. Phillip Johnson's painful memories of the Action Group
for Better Architecture's failed attempts in New York to protest
the demolition of Pennsylvania Station inspired a renewed effort.
Jackie fully understood the architectural history of New York's lost
landmarks and the sheer magnitude of the two year effort to topple
the old train station carved in stone and marble. While she was a
member of MAS, and an editor at Doubleday, she commissioned
David Garrard Lowe's *Stanford White's New York*.

With impeccable timing, Jacqueline Onassis' public support
to save Grand Central Terminal popularized the most important
ideological dispute in the history of the Municipal Art Society and
the Landmarks Commission's most ferocious legal battle to date.
The landmark law was originally designed to protect the preservation of historic districts, for example Greenwich Village, but MAS
extended the law to include single buildings located in commercial business districts, that would include Grand Central Terminal. The Municipal Art Society entered the Grand Central Terminal lawsuit as a friend of the court, and its brief bore the names of
some of the city's most influential legal and political minds. The
trial between the British developer, Morris Saady united with the

railroad's owner, Penn Central against the City of New York's Landmarks Commission was held in 1972. Months passed, then years, and still no decision was handed down by Judge Irving H. Saypol

Judge Saypol, looking back, "wished he'd never got mixed up in it . . . and wished it would just go away." In the fall of 1974, Kent Barwick, the new president of MAS, heard a decision was imminent, and asked to see the City Planning Commission's file on the case, so that some terrible news wouldn't arrive unexpected. On top of the bulging file sat the newest entry, a confidential memo to Mayor Beame. It reported that Judge Saypol had decided against New York City and the Landmarks Commission, and that the railroad's lawyers were offering a deal. If the city didn't appeal, Penn Central wouldn't sue for damages. If it did appeal, the railroad would demand $60 million. Mayor Beame was advised to drop the case against the railroad.

The news of Saypol's decision hit MAS like a cyclone uprooting a tiny mid-Western plains city. If Saypol's decision stood, the historic districts might still survive, but the whole category of individual landmarks, MAS's greatest contribution to the preservation movement—would be obliterated. The situation was critical, it called for the city to launch the most aggressive appeal, but the society had little confidence that this would happen. The head attorney for the city, Corporate Counsel Burke privately believed that the landmarks law was unconstitutional, and so did the chief of his appeals division. Mayor Beame had never supported landmarks preservation and with the vision of an accountant would support any developer who generated tax dollars to the city's coffers. For $60 million he just might gut the whole landmarks law.

Judge Saypol finally handed down his decision in February 1975. "I'll never forget that day as long as I live," a stunned Laurie Beckelman observes. The *Times* carried a front page article quoting Kent Barwick. Laurie Beckelman, operating as a one women deputy for all MAS departments, and Barwick created a plan to put as much pressure on the city not to drop the case. MAS quietly warned City Hall that they considered the survival of Grand

Central Terminal as a life-or-death issue. The society organized the Citizens Committee to Save Grand Central, and reconvened its lawyers' committee to plot the legal strategy for an appeal.

The tiny offices of MAS seemed to be an outpost under siege, as Barwick and Beckelman manned the phones that would not stop ringing. Suddenly, a women called, claiming to be Jacqueline Onassis, and asked to speak with Kent Barwick. Beckelman recalls the story in sheer disbelief, "If it was really Mrs. Onassis, why would she be calling herself?" Barwick took the call, and Onassis asked what she could do to support his efforts. He asked her to join the Citizens Committee to Save Grand Central, and within one year she had a seat on MAS's board of directors.

It makes perfect sense when you reconstruct her understanding of preserving Washington's architecture during the White House years. Her activism as first lady to create the legal status of the White House as a museum, the redevelopment of historic buildings in Washington D.C, and the fact that her Fifth Avenue apartment's view of Central Park was preserved by Frederick Law Olmstead, gives credence to her phone call that day.

Every magazine and newspaper in America and Europe reported Jackie's involvement with Grand Central. Suddenly it mattered as a national and international issue, but there were the cynics who cried, "it was just the hobby of people who never rode the subway." Yet, her involvement brought to MAS a visceral belief in preservation and ultimately far outweighed the negative droning of a few naysayers. Above all, she attracted news cameras, as if America's greatest movie star had offered to play her most revered role once again. People hesitated to rebuff her, and most importantly, when she made a phone call, it was returned. Even Mayor Beame was persuaded and as Beckelman remembers, "A nicely placed phone call from Jacqueline Onassis may have been what finally convinced the mayor to file the appeal."

"Grand Central Terminal as a railroad station works superbly," Jackie observes. "The originality and durability of its design solutions still leave transportation planners awe struck. As architecture it continues to give solace. Let us salute it for what it had meant in the past and for what it has done for the future."

The Oyster Bar press conference was Jackie's way to announce her steadfast belief in the battle that lie ahead: "I think this is so terribly important," Mrs. Onassis said, barely rising her voice over a whisper, "We've all heard that it's too late," she said facing the television cameras in a two-piece tan dress, "the public has been told that it has to happen, but we know it's not true. Even in the eleventh hour it's not too late." Mrs. Onassis explained that she chose to help save Grand Central because, "old buildings are important, and if we don't care about our past, then we can not have any hope for our future." Mrs. Onassis sounded the call to arms when she closed with the warning, "And I know that's what we'll do."

Fred Papert describes the smaller battles on the road to save Grand Central. With a firm voice, he proclaimed that Brendon Gill and Jackie, "led an army of preservationists and the citizens of America as they marched against the fall of Grand Central." Fred Papert's genius for publicity was behind many of Jackie's public appearances. On the train Landmark Express to Washington to hear the Supreme Court's final decision, Senator Daniel Patrick Moynihan, Jacqueline Onassis and other celebrities caused a whirlwind of publicity. Papert states, "And the justices were very impressed with the public interest in saving Grand Central, and that goes right to Onassis' credit." The New York press seemed to love every moment of her efforts to preserve Park Avenue's Lever House, especially when she reportedly gave a kiss that saved Lever House. Jackie lead the Stand Against the Shadow rally of preservationists including her friends Candace Bergen and I.M. Pei holding 'umbrellas in protest against the Columbus Circle skyscraper" as she cried to reporters, "they're stealing the sky". With Brendon Gill as her co-conspirator, their opposition to demolish St. Bartholomew's community house landed the blandishments of the parish's reverend, "just two architectural idolaters". She became beloved by New Yorkers when she boarded Landmark Express II on a journey to Albany to fight the demolition of St. Bartholomew's community house.

In May of 1982, Jacqueline Onassis wrote in The New York Historical Society's exhibition catalog to commemorate the Grand Central photography exhibition: "Let us now praise Grand Central Terminal. When the Committee to Save Grand Central was formed in 1975 it was joined by supporters from all over the country. When the Supreme Court ruled in its favor, it saved for us, in its original state, the majestic building which has a place in so many people's memories, so many people's lives."

Jackie's tales from another era stir our memories, giving us a nostalgic reason to preserve the buildings we grew up loving. In a girlish letter she once wrote, "I came up with a Hollywood producer, at least I sat next to him in the diner . . . and the last time it was a talent scout . . . and I do think one of them might have said . . . we could use you in pictures Lady! His name was J.F. Kennedy—the F. was for Fishbein because he thought he owed that to his family. He told me his picture was going to have its premiere at the United Nations but no one knew and I mustn't let it leak to the press.." Funny, no one seems to know whatever happened to J. Fishbein Kennedy's movie premiere. The friend who received this letter, wondered if it was just Jack Kennedy playing a little joke before Jackie knew him.

The young girl who traveled so often from Washington's Union Station to New York's Grand Central to visit her father Jack Bouvier, was the ultimate spokesperson to argue the case to preserve America's architectural treasures. She wrote: "New York City is the center of civilization as Athens, Rome, Persepolis were in theirs. Her citizens have recognized that by banding together they can save its loved buildings from destruction. From a young couple painstakingly renovating a brownstone, to artists fighting to keep old warehouses as studios, to workman redoing the cast iron bridges in Central Park, to the Municipal Art Society saving the Villard Houses and installing in them the situation room of urban planning, we see the preservationists effort here gather momentum as it has throughout the country."

IMPRESSIONS OF INDIA

Yusha Auchincloss loaned me *The Strategy of Peace*, and *A Princess Remembers, The Memoirs of the Maharani of Jaipur*. India's cultural traditions decorate the village streets, and Jackie traveled to this festive country on both personal and professional occasions. As a book editor, Jackie journeyed to India in 1985 to research Naveen Patnaik's exhibition catalog for The Costume Institute's exhibition *A Second Paradise: Indian Courtly Life, 1590-1947*. Naveen Patnaik once wrote, "Dear Jackie, traditionally people come to India in search of their gurus. It was my good fortune that my guru came to India. In every sense this book, *A Second Paradise*, is a tribute to you." The second book with Patnaik, a former governor in India, *The Garden of Life*, describes the healing aspects of Indian arts and ancient herbs and flowers.

Jackie's private library was stocked with endless books about Indian culture, history, art books about Mughal miniature paintings, philosophy and exquisitely illustrated rare volumes. A short list includes: Jawaharlal Nehru's *Toward Freedom* published in 1958. President Radhakrishnan's philosophy books were given to the Kennedys after his White House visit including *Indian Philosophy, Religion and Society, East and West, An Idealist View of Life, My Search For Truth*. Harvard's expert in Indian art, Stuart Cary Welch's books included *Indian Drawings and Painted Sketches, Gods Thrones and Peacocks, Room For Wonder*, and *A Flower From Every Meadow*. Other notable art history books by Indian scholar M. S. Randhawa are titled *Kangra Valley Painting* and *Basohli Painting*.

The Memoirs of the Maharani of Jaipur is a unique 20th century journey into the past of India through the life of the Maharani of Jaipur. A woman destined to become the voice of her people, however unprepared for the fierce duality of political life. When faced with devastating challenges in her life, she discovers her full powers, and makes a noble contribution to the modern history of India. Through her profound determination, she maintained the affection of her people.

The autobiography is also the story of one of Jackie's hosts from her visit to India in 1962. The two women remained life long friends, and Jackie often visited Jaipur on private trips to India during her life. The people, their customs, religion and their leaders' struggles maintain a special place in her heart. As a private citizen, she traveled to India to visit Daniel Patrick Moynihan while he was the Ambassador to India. The Harvard scholar Stuart Carey Welsh guided her later tours to India and she continued to study the country's history of art and religion.

The images of Jackie gliding along the Ganges River in 1962 during her goodwill tour of the country were broadcast all over India. The huge success of the landmark journey salutes Kennedy's Ambassador to India, John Kenneth Galbraith. The Ambassador and his wife Kitty suggested the idea to President Kennedy, and persuaded him to send Jackie on a highly publicized goodwill mission to India and Pakistan. At the time of her 1962 goodwill trip, the threat of communist Red China was looming over India, but Jackie's trip was wisely proclaimed by the Ambassador as unofficial, non-political.

John Kenneth Galbraith described an episode before Jackie arrived in India: "My wife Kitty and I planned Jacqueline Kennedy's trip to India. We resisted a proposal that she visit the ancient temples of Konarak, where her viewing of explicitly erotic statuary would have greatly attracted media attention. President Kennedy's reply to his wife viewing sensuous statuary was, "Don't you think she's old enough?" Galbraith remarks, "We were her host and hostess until Jawaharlal Nehru snatched her away from us." As the distinguished Ambassador has often remarked, "It was an occasion for everyone to have a good time." The journey was filmed by dozens of reporters, including the young Barbara Walters, and the United States Information Agency. As the stories filtered back to America, it was widely reported that in India, Jacqueline Kennedy, was hailed as "Durga, Goddess of Power."

A special guest among the press corps was the French native painter Jacqueline Duhême. Duhême, a friend of Matisse, Picasso and Eluard, intrigued President Kennedy after he saw her paintings of the Kennedy's Paris trip in June of 1961. "I think everyone was absolutely overwhelmed by the radiant charm and simplicity of Jack and Jackie Kennedy. To us, in France, the image of world politics is something a bit more austere." When Jacqueline Kennedy planned her trip to India, she invited Duhême to paint the daily scenes taking place so that *McCall's* magazine could publish the paintings to illustrate the journey. Duhême is the only 20th century artist who has traveled as a painter-journalist on international diplomatic missions with Charles De Gaulle to South America and Jacqueline Kennedy to India.

Jackie's trip to India seemed to be a graceful way to celebrate two different cultures and religions. En route to India with her sister, Princess Lee Radziwill, the wife of America's first Catholic President stopped in Rome for an audience with Pope John XXIII. "Che bella!" cheered a thousand Romans gathered at the airport to welcome the stylish first lady dressed in a Somali leopard-skin coat and a black mink pillbox hat. Jacqueline Kennedy arrived in Rome to pay homage to the eighty-year old Pontiff.

On the Sunday morning of March 11, 1962, the thirty-two year old first lady in a full-length black dress of heavy silk, long black gloves and a Spanish mantilla of black lace that covered all but her face, was to meet one of the most powerful religious leaders in the world. Mrs. Kennedy was received by the diminutive Pope John XXIII who conversed with her in his Vatican library for thirty-two minutes. The first lady and the Pope spoke only in French since he was not fluent in English. He gave her rosaries and medals of his Pontificate, and she gave him a personally inscribed copy of President Kennedy's speeches. A Catholic by birth, she was visibly moved by her private meeting and especially honored when a mass was offered for her. The Pope received other members of her party, with the exception of Princess Lee Radziwill, who was divorced.

The next day, March 12th, at the New Delhi airport, Jacqueline Kennedy and Princess Radziwill were greeted by Prime Minister Jawaharlal Nehru, his daughter Indira Gandhi and the American Ambassador to India, John Kenneth Galbraith. Nehru, a great admirer of the lovely first lady, left Parliament to greet his guests. On the long road to New Delhi, one hundred thousand people, including peasants and villagers in bullock carts parked wheel to wheel lined the wide streets of the capital to hail the "Amriki Raini!" Jacqueline and Lee stopped to watch the formal procession of President Rajendra Prasad as he left Parliament in a regal black and gold landau drawn by six sorrel horses and guarded by seventeen outriders in scarlet coats and enormous turbans.

Some time before the American Bouvier sisters tour of India, the Maharani of Jaipur, Gayatri Devi, known informally as Ayesha, with the support of her husband the Maharaja of Jaipur, Sawai Man Singh, nicknamed Jai, ran for Parliament in the new government and so did his two sons Pat and Joey. The Maharaja of Jaipur, Sawai Man Singh, was already a member of the Upper House of Parliament. The royal Indian families knew it would be necessary to secure their family's traditional role as parents or guardians to their people to transfer power from the aristocrats to the poor, secure the representation for their people in the new government and guarantee that the tax structure of the princely states would not be harmed by the new government.

In 1947, when India became a free nation, and democracy ended the rule of the independent princely states, the former royal families ran for Parliament in order to continue to represent and provide for their provinces. When first time candidate, the Maharani of Jaipur, was campaigning for the Lower House of Parliament, the Maharaja of Jaipur, Ayesha's husband gave his unconditional support to his wife and sons. In the gardens of the Royal Palace, he gave this speech:

"For generations," Jai addressed the huge gathering of his people in the traditional tu as a father to his children, "my family have ruled you, and we have built up many generations of affection. The new government has taken my state from me, but for all I care they can take the shirt off my back as long as I can keep that bond of trust and affection. They accuse me of putting up my wife and two of my sons for election. They say that if I had a hundred and seventy-six sons, that being the number of electoral seats in Rajasthan Assembly, that I would put them all up too, but they don't know, do they," and with his arm he waved to his people in a confidential gesture, "that I have far more than one hundred and seventy-six sons!"

The audience of over 200,000 Indians roared with cheers. Ayesha describes the scene, "Then the people, in high excitement and joy, threw flowers at us, and we threw them back in a mood of spontaneous gaiety. That was the moment at which I knew that I would be elected."

The Maharaja and the Maharani of Jaipur were leaders of the Swatantra Party. The political party appealed to intellectuals, attorneys and the well-educated with a liberal mantra to lift the poor into true freedom through education. One of her main problems was educating an largely illiterate population of women how to vote. The women were instructed to mark the proper symbol of the Swatantra Party, a star, so that a vote could be counted in her favor. The women could not understand why there was no symbol for the Maharaja. They thought if her symbol was a star then his must be the sun. But if they marked both a star for the Swatantra Party and a sun for an opposing party, then the vote would be invalid.

As a member of the royal family, the Maharani of Jaipur, Ayesha was born to a wealthy family, educated in the best English schools and lived a life of great luxury, shopping and traveling abroad. She was accustomed to the freedoms of modern women, but her most serious activity as the wife of a prince was to protect the religious life of her children and her husband. Polygamy was widely practiced in India, and Ayesha was the third and last woman to marry the Maharaja of Jaipur. An ancient social custom, purdah, cloistering the wives of princes and wealthy men, deeply offended Ayesha. On the day of her election, she witnessed the uninhibited joy of her people. Her experience was an awakening that changed her life forever. Women dressed in fine clothes walked with their husbands and children, singing along the way, to vote in the village. Farmers arrived in bull-carts decorated with flowers and bright colors of cloth, the animals garlanded, to be greeted by entertainers, storytellers, and sweets-vendors. Everyone was on holiday until the election votes had been counted.

When the results of her election were announced, she had won by a majority of over 175,000 votes. The Jaipur family appears in the 1963 *Guinness Book of World Records* for two events. First for having the most expensive wedding in the world, secondly for Ayesha's election, which was at the time the largest majority won by any candidate running for office in any democratic country in the world. Upon hearing this news of her victory, her husband and the people of Jaipur were elated. Ayesha's mother observes, "How lucky you are to have a husband who backs you up in everything. Can you believe that some men are jealous of their wives?" Ayesha confessed to her husband Jai, "I have never felt so greatly loved."

Maharaja of Jaipur's sons, Pat won a seat in the lower house, and Joey won in the State Assembly. The political climate in Delhi at that moment was controlled by the ruling Congress Party with 300 of the 535 seats in Parliament. The Opposition comprised of the Swatantra Party included differing political groups; the extreme right-wing Jana Sangh Hindu party, the Socialists and the largest was the Communist Party.

Ayesha spoke about this moment in her life as absolutely absorbing. She remarks, "I made a special point of attending when Pandit Nehru was speaking, he was in charge of the future of our country and all of us." Suddenly, the Maharani of Jaipur received a message in New Delhi that First Lady Jacqueline Kennedy and Princess Radziwill accepted her invitation to visit Jaipur. Ayesha left New Delhi to prepare for her American friends' arrival.

Jacqueline Kennedy and Princess Radziwill's itinerary included traveling through India commencing in New Delhi, on board President Prasad's train, to adventures in Fatehpor, Sikri, Agra, Benares, Udaipur, Jaipur, and in Pakistan; Lahore, Rawalpindi, Peshawar, Karachi, and Teheran. After Jackie and Lee visited Udaipur one of India's most magnificent cities, and the capital of the northwestern Indian state Rajhastan known as "the land of the kings", they planned to travel to Jaipur to see Ayesha. A dramatic boat journey on Lake Pichola was arranged to visit the exquisite White Palace on an island in the middle of the lake. Jackie's visit to the palace, angered the leaders of the Congress Party in Delhi. American Ambassador John Kenneth Galbraith was warned that the Kennedy entourage appeared to be too 'friendly' with the royal families.

In Jaipur, Ayesha told the American Ambassador that, "quite naturally, our sightseeing program will include a visit to the City Palace. With Jackie's interest in art, she must see the Jaipur collection and Jai's ancestral home." On the second day of her visit, Jai and Ayesha planned to take her to the City Palace. Jackie objected, "But Ayesha, I've been told that I'm not allowed to go there." The American Ambassador informed Jackie that a public visit might offend the Congress government in New Delhi. Ayesha recalls, "It seemed too silly to believe, but all the same, Mr. Galbraith, who accompanied Jackie to Jaipur, had to make a long telephone call to consult with Congress leaders in Delhi before Jackie was allowed to go to the City Palace." Jackie was granted permission to see the City Palace at night with only Jai and Ayesha as her escorts.

In Agra, Jackie strolled past the cypresses along the Taj Mahal's water gardens reflecting a spectacle of the shimmering white marble mausoleum. She told the press, in her soft voice, "I am overwhelmed by a sense of awe. I have seen pictures of the Taj, but for the first time I am struck with a sense of its mass and symmetry." She returned later that evening to see the Taj by moonlight. One reporter wrote that, "she looked so young, simple unaffected against the extraordinary beauty of the doomed Taj and its four graceful minarets . . ." The Taj Mahal built in the seventeenth century over a period of twenty-two years, under the direction of the grand-son of Mogul Emperor Akbar, Shah Jahan, pays homage to his beloved queen, Mumtaz Mahal.

The presidential train brought the first lady from Agra to the holy city of Benares, one of the oldest cities still inhabited along the Ganges River. On that hot morning, Lee and Jacqueline boarded a boat garlanded with marigolds to view the bathing areas and cremation platforms along the riverside. Scarlet-liveried bearers sheltered both women with great parasols as large crowds gathered along the river banks blowing deafening blasts on conch shells while tapping on triangles in excitement and admiration. After the ride on the Ganges River, Jacqueline walked up a petal strewn path to Sarnath Stupa, the temple from which the Buddha preached his first sermon two thousand five hundred years ago.

Nehru remarked that the American visit "added greatly to the psychological pull" of friendship between his country and the United States. The journey did not include a visit to Pakistan, but President Ayub Khan's invitation could not be refused. On March 22nd, the first lady arrived in Lahore, Pakistan to showers of flower petals, drums, bursting balloons.

That evening President Khan accompanied her on a stroll through the fabled Shalimar Gardens. Jackie, wearing the traditional welcoming tinsel garland, greeted seven thousand guests, mostly women, waiting in the gardens to see the American First Lady. She told her admirers, "All my life, I have dreamed of coming to Shalimar Gardens. Now, as I stand here in these beautiful gardens that were built long before my country was born, I know that my own countrymen have a pride in its culture too. And that's just one more thing that binds us together, and always will."

When Jackie returned to Washington D.C. she invited the Maharaja and the Maharani of Jaipur to visit the White House when Ayesha could arranged the visit. By October of 1962, Ayesha and Jai arrived in New York City as the Cuban Missile Crisis erupted on the national evening news, unleashing a frenzy of fears. Instead of abandoning plans to travel to Washington, they braved the threats, and stuck to their plans.

On October 20, 1962, Theodore Sorensen, during the Cuban Missile Crisis, recalled an afternoon meeting with President Kennedy and the Attorney General Robert Kennedy. On the second story terrace facing the panorama of the Potomac River, the Lincoln Memorial and Arlington: "He (JFK) showed no signs of either frenzy or despair . . . his commands were crisp and clear . . . I returned to my office in the West Wing of the White House to work on the new speech draft . . . immeasurably cheered by his good humor, warned by his deep feeling, inspired by his quiet strength . . ."

The dance and dinner in honor of India was canceled. But, President Kennedy insisted that a small dinner for his guests take place. "I hear you are the Barry Goldwater of India," announced President Kennedy smiling at the victorious Ayesha. Senator Goldwater, a popular conservative from Arizona, won his recent election with a large majority. At dinner, Kennedy told Jai and Ayesha how impressed he had been with Rajaji, Pandit Nehru's Prime Minister. Rajaji joined major nations to support the Nuclear Disarmament Conference in Washington. Kennedy said to Ayesha, "I was expecting an old man dressed in white and talking pompous nonsense . . . but instead I was impressed by Rajaji's wisdom and lucidity." Kennedy admired Rajaji so much that his aides had to drag him away for his next appointment.

Ayesha found President Kennedy an immensely attractive personality, with boyish looks and manners, and with such an infectious smile she told her husband, "I found it difficult to remember at times that he was the President of the United States."

The following day, Jackie gave Ayesha and Jai a tour of the restored White House. As they strolled through the Rose Garden, they heard the President calling out from the Oval Office, inviting Ayesha to meet some of her comrades. The Indian princess, a regal beauty moved gracefully, as if dressed in a floating sari. Her delicate visage shocked an imposing group of Senators, when the President announced, "here is the women with the most staggering majority that anyone has ever earned in an election."

The Maharaja and the Maharani of Jaipur departed for New York, and were immediately notified that war had broken out between Red China and India. The Indian army had suffered heavy casualties and were vastly outnumbered by the Red Chinese forces. The fighting was near Ayesha's ancestral home of Cooch Behar, the north-east border of India.

When they arrived in Delhi, the Red Chinese had crossed India's north-eastern frontier, easily crushing the poorly-trained Indian army unprepared for high altitude warfare in the treacherous terrain of the Himalayas. Jai and Ayesha returned to Parliament to witness a furious debate about the unwarranted invasion. The outrage over the invasion developed into an investigation into Pandit Nehru's foreign policy allowing the Indian people to believe the Red Chinese had only fraternal feelings for India. Nehru was widely quoted as saying, "Indians and Chinese are brothers."

Ayesha was so angered by this revelation that she stood before Parliament and said to Nehru, "If you had known anything about anything, we wouldn't be in this mess today." Nehru replied that he had not heard the lady's words, and carried on. The members of Parliament cried out "Chivalry!" in mocking tones. So she repeated herself, and Nehru replied, "I will not bandy words with a lady!"

During this crisis, Nehru turned to Khrushchev, whom he had regarded as a friend and backer. The answer from Moscow was that India should accept the Chinese offer to cease-fire in exchange for the Red China's military control of a more advantageous region inside the borders of India. Russia's calculated alliance with Communist China stung Nehru, forcing him to request the support of President Kennedy and Great Britain. Both countries sent military aid, and Kennedy advised Nehru to tell Khrushchev, "to put up or shut up." Nehru concluded never to trust the Chinese again, and the Indian people cheered all signs of United States military supplies.

In 1963, the Senate approved President Kennedy's atmospheric Nuclear Test Ban Treaty over opposition from Barry Goldwater, the popular senator from Arizona, and a majority of military leaders. On October 7, 1963 President Kennedy performed a ceremony that gave him the deepest personal satisfaction of his three years in the White House, the signing of the formal ratification of the treaty between the three nuclear powers, the United States, England and the Soviet Union. The Nuclear Test Ban Treaty prohibited atomic testing, "on the atmosphere, in outer space, and in the deep underwater oceans." The treaty was agreed upon and signed by Averell Harriman, Lord Hailsham and Andrei Gromyko, and one hundred and two nations eventually joined the other countries. The ratification ceremony was held in the Treaty Room, where the Peace Protocol ending the Spanish-American War had been signed in 1898. President Kennedy remarked that the Nuclear Test Ban Treaty gave him the greatest personal satisfaction knowing this agreement provided a tangible hope that other nation's desire to preserve peace would survive.

The Chinese invasion of India created new alliances among the Indian political party system ultimately dismantling the constitutional rights granted to the royal families. After Jawaharlal Nehru died in 1964, and Indira Ghandi became the Prime

Minister the situation grew worse. Then the Maharaja of Jaipur died playing polo in England on June 26, 1970. Prince Phillip, a great friend of Jai's wrote to Ayesha, "He combined a very rare quality in men, and he was supremely civilized. Kind and modest, but with an unerring instinct for the highest standards of human ambition and behavior." Memorial services were held in Jaipur and in England. Ayesha was devastated and retreated into isolation.

The jockeying of power in India erupted into an attack on the royal families' special tax called the privy purse. In 1947, the friendly relations of the royal families in England and India fostered the crucial path that opened the way to freedom for India. As the Maharaja of Jaipur, Jai had influenced his friend 'Dicky' Mountbatten, Lord of Burma, close friends with the Queen and Prince Phillip to support a free India. A short time after Jai's death, Ayesha heard the news that the central government was challenging more than the right to collect the tax, a privy purse, but the constitutional rights of the royal families' titles. Ayesha was astonished and left for New Delhi.

Once hailed as "the co-architects of Indian freedom," the Concord of Princes was according the central government, the most progressive influence in liberating the Indian people from British rule in 1947. The Maharani of Jaipur felt that the daughter of the revered reformer Mrs. Ghandi's chief goal should be to liberate the Caste System. For centuries, Ayesha reasoned, legislated slavery divided Indian society restricting the economic freedom of the most disadvantaged people. The warning signs were unclear to the royal families, and Prime Minister Indira Ghandi prevailed over the Concord of Princes. In 1971, the Twenty-sixth Amendment of the Constitution was introduced into Parliament. During the debate, the Prime Minister, Indira Ghandi, spoke of abolishing class divisions and class distinction. "We may be depriving the princes of luxury, but we are giving them the opportunity to be men."

Naveen Patnaik observes in *A Second Paradise: Indian Courtly Life*, "Over five hundred Indian kingdoms had voluntarily signed away ancestral homes and sovereign rights to spare their people

the anguish of civil war. With that last great gesture of royal mag-
nanimity they ended the fabled era of India's courts and kingdoms." For the next forty years, political life in India remained
uncertain. Prime Minister Indira Ghandi lost her next election. In
1976, Mrs. Ghandi published *Freedom Is the Starting Point* observing that, "Mankind will endure when the world appreciates the
logic of diversity." She regained her position in 1980, then was
assassinated in 1985. The turmoil in India did not diminish the
image of a young Jacqueline Kennedy, rather her memory evokes
sentimental nostalgia for a lasting American friendship. "The people
of India," John Kenneth Galbraith once remarked, "revered her."

During Nehru's first visit to the Kennedy White House, he
reminded Americans of India's deep commitment to peace. On
November 6, 1961 he addressed the President: "Among the things
that Mahatma Ghandi laid great stress on, as you no doubt know
Mr. President, was on peace and the peaceful methods of approach
to problems. Even in our struggle with the British Empire of those
days we adhered to peaceful methods. And so we are fortunate
that at the end of that struggle when we achieved freedom it was
with the friendship of the British people."

Many of the costumes in Naveen Patnaik's beautifully illustrated *A Second Paradise: Indian Courtly Life, 1590-1947* were loaned
from Jaipur's museums, and Ayesha's private collection. The very
last photograph in the book is one of Ayesha, a romantic black and
white portrait of the Maharaja Sawai Man Singh and his young
wife the Maharani Gayatri Devi taken in 1942 before India became a free country. Naveen Patnaik wrote, "In the final months of
their reigns many Indian rulers behaved as though nothing had
changed. In the evenings the gardens glowed with lamps, the fra-
grant incense filled the night and colored fountains played as
though time were standing still . . . singers and musicians, knowing that the days of royal patronage were drawing to a close, performed with a last moving brilliance." Patnaik adds that a contemporary poet captures the nostalgia:

The time has come for farewells
We cannot meet again except in dreams
But I shall be reminded of this world
When I find a faded flower
Pressed between the pages of a long forgotten book

The Garden of Life describes the healing medicines in Indian culture developed by an ancient people the Ayurveda. The ancient medical tradition hoped to "alleviate all human suffering." Naveen Patnaik describes the shift in attitude towards foreigners seeking a cultural adventure in India. When at one time, they sought out gurus and spiritual teachers, he observes, "Now they express a desire to know about Indian medicine." He wonders why the growing interest: "I began to realize their past interest in Indian spiritual views is not so different from the present curiosity about Indian medicine. This realization would hardly have surprised the men who founded Ayurveda thousands of years ago in the mountainous regions of the Himalayas. They did not separate the external world from man's inner world, nor did they isolate man's spiritual anguish from his other sufferings."

Jackie traveled to India almost annually as a guest of the Maharani of Jaipur and other friends. She sustained her friendship with Ayesha, and a fondness for all the royal families that were so gracious to her in 1962. One of Jackie's authors, Ruth Prawer Jhabvala once said, "India always changes people, and I am no exception." Jackie returned so often she seemed to thrive on the air, discovering some magical elixir in India's culture and customs.

PETER SIS AFTER THE VELVET REVOLUTION

Jackie regularly conducted scholarly research before making a final commitment to an author. At The New York Public Library, she spent endless weeks in the private library of the Baltic and Slavic Division researching Russian and Eastern European documents and photographs. Jackie and one of her authors Peter Sis seemed lost in the midst of deciphering what book to create and his stories inspired her 'research trip' to his beloved homeland Czechoslovakia. President Vaclav Havel offered to act as private host for her last official research journey to Prague.

Doubleday's associate publisher, Marly Rusoff, said "Peter Sis was someone she was very interested in for months before they did a book together." His illustrated journey books are decorative fairytale stories targeted for young readers. Peter Sis observed "that Mrs. Onassis felt a book like mine, a history mixed with dreams both realized and forgotten might appeal to more sophisticated readers." Jackie's long list of social contacts, including former presidents and famous diplomats, distinguished authors, dancers and singers would make it an herculean effort to search for a new name. Did she ever 'discover' someone new, someone she didn't know? Doubleday published an insightful memorial tribute listing each book Jackie edited, and some tearful stories from a selection of her authors. There were many history volumes on Russia and France, and the performing arts, but how did Jackie discover Christine

Zamoyska Panek who wrote *Have You Forgotten: A Memoir of Poland, 1939–1945*. Marly Rusoff said Jackie was definitely open to new writers then suggested I talk to Peter Sis.

Marly Rusoff handed me a magazine and said, "Here, Peter Sis, a Czechoslovakian author and illustrator, came to Jackie's attention in the May/June 1991 issue of *Print* magazine. He designed the cover with one of his painted eggs." After our meeting, as I looked through the magazine, lingering over an advertisement for Jaguar, these words popped off the page, "Did anyone ever tell you, you look just like John F. Kennedy?" Then there was a long article titled *The Death of Eros*. Bert Stern's photographs of Marilyn Monroe taken six weeks before her death on August 5, 1962 define modern sensuality. How strange it must have been for Jackie to have such sensitive memories, her husband's handsome looks and Marilyn Monroe's legacy, appear while looking for the article on Peter Sis a few pages later.

Peter tells the story, "She contacted me through my agency. She saw the cover I did for *Print* magazine with a painted egg. So, I went to see her with my portfolio."

At the time, the author/illustrator was at work on a book to celebrate the 500th anniversary of Christopher Columbus. "I was working on a lot of medieval looking maps." Jackie told Peter, "I wish this was my book." Illustrated with psychedelic watercolor paintings styled after 'pointillism', Sis' books evoke the intricate beauty of ancient illuminated manuscripts. Jackie introduced Peter Sis to the Rare Map Division at The New York Public Library and gave him several suggestions on how to find old maps to study.

The editor was intrigued with Sis, and he recalls her interest, "One thing puzzling to me was that she was one of the few people who looked at all my films and theater designs." Jackie screened his animation films, his children's books and pre-American posters from his past. "I mean there are some editors who just concentrate on books. I would tell them I did some animation but they didn't care. She really look at everything very carefully."

Peter observes, "It was amazing, I spoke about a book I liked when I was a child, then we talk about Greece, on to China's arts and then poetry. She was wonderful. She thought the way we did in Europe or like my father. Because with my father I had a special language. We would just have one word that's the signal and then we would know what we are talking about. I had the same feeling with Mrs. Onassis. I call it flying, we would start flying, weaving the dreams together."

The idea to illustrate a fairytale originating in Peter Sis' homeland Czechoslovakia had often been rejected. When he first met Jackie, he said: "I did not dare to bring up Prague, the place I grew up. My experience was that no one cared or knew about it."

Prague, until the city's reawakening during the 1989 Velvet Revolution, was relegated to obscurity. To the artists grave frustration most editors seemed geographically confused and would often reply, "Where is it?" or "Why not Paris?" or "Why not Venice?" or even, "Why not Moscow?"

Jackie said to him, "Why didn't you ever think about doing a book about Prague?"

Peter told her, "I did, I did!"

And then she offered, "So do it!"

Peter, after growing up in a Communist controlled society, remembers feeling scared. Suddenly, a forbidden freedom to realize a treasured dream inspired his next book.

Then, without telling Peter Sis, in 1991, Jacqueline Onassis and Maurice Tempelsman traveled to Prague to meet President Vaclav Havel. Havel's prominence rekindles the flames of an old debate: who is best suited to serve a democracy the intellectual or the politician, or must the public servant possess the best talents of both. Vaclav Havel's transformation from playwright to president was fraught with the devastating effects of a twenty-one year totalitarian regime. In 1968, Soviet tanks crushed the Prague Spring, and mobilized a Communist government. Havel's plays of the 1960s, *The Garden Party, The Memorandum, The Increased Difficulty of Concentration*, are political satires illuminating the dehumanizing effects of the 20th century's industrialized bureaucracies. His 1984 play *Largo Desolato* depicts the overwhelming burden of a dissident intellectual frustrated with his people's unyielding expectations of his role as eternal provider of hope. Havel observes: "Obviously concerns for public affairs means a concern for humanity . . . And that requires that a recognition of all aspects of our self-awareness in the world . . . I do not see how a politician can achieve that without recognizing the dramatic element is an inherent aspect of the world . . . thus a fundamental tool of human communication . . ."

It was intensely symbolic for President Vaclav Havel that the political group of intellectuals, the Civic Forum, responsible for the 1989 Velvet Revolution's master plan, invented a new Czech democracy in a theater prophetically named The Magic Lantern. The Velvet Revolution liberated Havel from prison, and he was elected president. Vaclav Havel's moral authority is rooted in ethical and spiritual values, and in the vital role of future leaders to be responsible for the needs of all people in a local community and the larger world: "We must stop seeing ourselves as masters of the universe . . . who can do whatever occurs to us. We must discover a new respect for what transcends us; for the universe; for the earth; for nature; for life, for religion and for reality. Our respect for other people, other nations and other cultures, can only grow from a humble respect for the cosmic order and that we are a part of it."

She called Peter to describe her sightseeing tour. To Peter's delight she knew the names of all the Baroque architects. "She really surprised me, because she was really into Prague architecture. She knew about the Baroque architects, the ancient Jewish temple, and the houses. She knew the names of the sculptures on the Charles Bridge and studied the mixing of the cultures like the German and Czech culture and the Jewish culture and Italian architects. It was a small melting pot of Europe, and she was interested in how many amazing people came to Prague."

Remembering
Mrs. Onassis

A Memoir by Peter Sis

Jackie and Peter settled on the idea of *The Three Golden Keys*. The concept for the book included quotes from famous people who had visited Prague. One quote struck both of them as both lyrical and the perfect metaphor for the book: "Oh, I know my little mother. I know my little mother Prague really well. The heart always keeps the deepest secrets and there are many secrets in these old houses." Peter revealed that the book addressed his personal feelings for his mother. He sketched seventy black and white images, hoping that they would select half for the book. When he presented the drawings to her, she was so thrilled she said, "Okay let's do the whole thing."

Peter was alarmed because he felt he needed more time to conceptualize the book. "That was a big trouble because I was happy that I was so free, but I realized I can't do it in four or five months. He told Jackie, "You know this is becoming a major project!"

And she said, "You just take all the time you need."

The deadline went from April 1992, to July, then August and then she called Peter and said, "What's happening with our book?"

As he worked on the illustrations, Peter described how he was submerged into his childhood that was sometimes threatening, and many times his memories were filled with dark feelings: "It was not a cheerful spring-like place. There were some wonderful moments, but it was always a little scary, a little medieval. And the way I did it and put it on the walls, I just got to the point when I couldn't move on anymore. And in the same time, I was undergoing a deep depression just because I was in this studio on Lafayette Street in Soho and it wasn't a big space. And all of a sudden it was surrounding me. So, all of a sudden, all these dark memories filtered into the undertone in the book. Prague was always a little spooky for me."

Peter told Jackie what was going on with the book: "And in that moment, it was quite magical that she came downtown to my studio and gave me the little kick I needed at that time." She said to me, "This is wonderful and keep on going."

"Prague is really a dark, dark memory for me. Heavy stones and grey autumn. Not, not blue sky and light, fresh green leaves."

Peter said to her, "These pictures will be on black paper and then it will be really spooky." She said, 'Okay, it will be on the black paper'. But I didn't know that she spoke to the art director, and they decided the pictures should be on beige paper, on sort of bark paper." Jackie oversaw the production quality of the book, selecting a printing house in Italy with elegant beige tone, beautiful paper. "I know as a matter of fact, that she wanted paper samples from all the printing houses around the world to see who would do the best job on the book."

Peter Sis' arrangement with Jackie was unique: "She was the only person I ever worked with who didn't ask how much is it going to cost and all the limitations of other work unfortunately I've been doing. Commercial art is always, what is the deadline, how much, what's the size, what's the age group, what are the limitations?" When he did ask her about these things, she told him not to worry about it.

Jackie was thrilled with *The Three Golden Keys* and hopeful they would create another book: "We dreamed of fairytale books about India, China and other ancient cultures." Peter remembers how she inspired him, "we talked about how you can make people better through beautiful books." Jackie often sent post-cards to Peter. Several times, he received a postcard depicting a painting that he was illustrating for *The Three Golden Keys*. "She once sent me a postcard from Stockholm of The Librarian, a painting by Guiseppe Arcimboldo belonging to Prague from the 17th century . . ." Jackie writes in her postcard, "Dear Peter, Look what I saw in Skoktoster Castle, taken as booty from Prague." Peter Sis was modeling the illustrations of the library in his book based on the exact same 17th century painting by Arcimboldo.

"And another postcard arrived from Avignon." Jackie sent Peter a postcard of a mural painting in an Avignon castle. Peter had the exact same picture stuck to the wall of his studio. "There were a few amazing visual esthetics we shared which was lovely."

There was one idea for a book they talked about over and over again, they both loved it. "We were always talking about this book which I love so much by Alain-Fournier about someone who travels with the circus and lives in a little village in France. It's very romantic. We were thinking this might be the next book. And then, there was this beautiful story written by a king in Provence. A good king Rene who travels on a trip around the world and tries to find decency and commitment and love and things like that." Over a few years, Peter and his editor considered books based on the themes in *The Baron in the Trees* by Italo Calvino, *Le Grand Meaulnes* by Alain-Fournier, a book about Tibet, and Jules Verne.

The Doubleday people advised Peter there would be some news about Mrs. Onassis' illness, but her doctors were optimistic. After a meeting in April of 1994 to discuss *The Three Golden Keys'* press release, a letter from Jackie arrived. "Your book is so magnificent. Each drawing looks into the well of an artist's mind and creativity, like nothing I have ever seen before."

"She really changed my world upside down which I'm grateful for. I once thought my own stories were more about my personal feelings of leaving your home and going to another country. But she somehow made me see that it's much less about poor me being somewhere else feeling sort of strange. And it's more about the human spirit of decency and civilization. What makes man different from the other species. Somehow tell it to future generations so we could keep it going. Change the egocentric observation into something much bigger."

"And I know what she's saying . . ." Peter Sis left Prague in 1981, struggling as a displaced émigré artist in America, "because I lived through Communism, and the Russian invasion and all kinds of terrible things. Now, I go to schools to talk to kids and when I say the Berlin Wall or the Russians coming to Prague in '68, the kids don't know what I'm talking about because it's over. It's wonderful now. So maybe just the beautiful thoughts and poets, filmmakers, painters will remain and we will forget about all the terrible stuff. If you look at the 20th century with all the political mischief, wars and murders, I believe, she will come out of it as some sort of wonderful angel."

AN AMERICAN AUTHOR:
LOUIS AUCHINCLOSS

Louis Auchincloss advised, "Jackie was unusual in that she actually liked the books she edited. Some editors, you must know, wouldn't want to read any of the books they publish." Louis Auchincloss' grand tour of his library included all sorts of wonderful French marriage documents from the 18th century. His voice lulled into a reverential wonder when he pointed out his complete leather bound edition of the diaries of the Duc de Saint Simon. I discovered one book I wanted to borrow, his wife's edition of Andre Malraux's *The Voices of Silence*. Both Yusha and Louis Auchincloss have wonderful private libraries filled with books that one will never find at The New York Public Library.

Jackie admired Louis, her cousin by marriage, when she was a young women. In 1951, after reading his novel *Sibyl*, she declared that her first engagement to the New York banker, John Husted, would mirror the dull, sad life of the main character in the novel. That marriage never occurred. Auchincloss recalls: "Yes, she had a private persona a good deal stronger than her public one which always shows her as kind of mild and talking in a very soft way." Auchincloss observed a much more resolute personality and that the strength of her character was betrayed by her beauty. She was a dazzling debutante, but even Louis Auchincloss recalls that, "Jackie was of course an extremely beautiful girl. But there were lots of beautiful girls around. You didn't expect a beautiful girl to become First Lady of the land or anything like that."

When Jackie became First Lady, Louis Auchincloss, a Republican, remained aloof, never pursuing the status of a White House prominent guests. Their friendship was rekindled years later when he agreed to write the social history of Versailles to accompany Deborah Turbeville's tour de force *Unseen Versailles.*

Jackie said to Louis when the book was nearly completed: "You're bad-mouthing our book all over New York!"

Mischief was his answer: "I've got the director talking, and he's telling tales about the book, but that's good publicity because everybody will buy it now!"

Louis, like a prophet-philosopher, confirms: "And a great many people did buy the book. That's when I learned what a careful editor she was; every single photograph that went into that book was chosen by her out of many others, and every bit of my text she went over with the greatest care, and she knew her French history extremely well."

Jackie discovered in Louis a shared devotion to the 18th century courts of Louis XIV. Her own tastes reflected, "the exquisite taste of the 18th century," Louis once remarked. He wrote a novel based on the famous Duc de Saint Simon diaries revealing his impressions of the court of the Sun King Louis XIV. Although Jackie was not his editor, Louis knew she studied the Duc de Saint Simon, and dedicated *The Cat and the King* to her.

False Dawn: Women in the Age of the Sun King was a history book Jackie worked on as the editor. Louis laments, "That laid an egg." The history book describes why women gained power through religious virtue, marriage, affairs and alliances with nobility and most often by the fate of their birth. The more well-born, the more power they held.

"It was called *False Dawn* because there were a series of very important women in France and England. England had two queens during the period of Louis XIV, Mary II and Queen Anne, and of course the women in the court of Louis XIV, Madame de Mantenon were considered the most powerful women in Europe. There was a whole series of others. It looked as if women were ready to come into their own. Granted they were all people who had enormous importance by their birth rather than by acquirement, still they were all women of tremendous talent."

History reveals the lives of these women merely opened the door to the vast inequities between the sexes. The luminating fact remained that once these women passed, the social customs did not change. There was no feminist reform movement in France in the 18th century. At that time, it was unthinkable, but they did inspire the idea that women had the abilities and the intelligence equal to men. Louis concludes, "There's a famous quote: 'Women reigned, then the French Revolution de-throned them.'"

"When we really started working together very closely was when I discovered a diary of my wife's Vanderbilt grandmother, Adele Sloan, who had been a debutante in New York during the 'Mauve Decade' the 1890's, and was related to the Vanderbilt family. She had a viewpoint as a women on that very lush extravaganza of an era that made the diary quite interesting. And I told Jackie that she was the only editor I know who could do a job on this—and she loved it!"

She told Louis, "People will want to buy the book for two reasons. They want a historical romance or a period piece to understand social history. Women like to read historical romances because they learn a lot of history painlessly while participating in a love story and identifying themselves with the heroine."

In 1982, Jackie wrote Louis Auchincloss a long letter in which she described her editorial revisions to transform the diary of the 1890's into a dramatic history. She had her doubts unless news events were added to place the life of Adele Sloan in exactly the right historical perspective.

For Jacqueline Kennedy Onassis,
who persuaded me that Versailles
was still a valid source for fiction.

LOUIS AUCHINCLOSS

The Cat
and the King

Charcoal drawing of Louis Auchincloss by Jack Beal

VERSAILLES

Jackie's editorial changes placed the diary in an historical
era, so that the social customs could be studied within the
framing of current world events. Jackie writes in her letter:
"Could you describe what was going on in the world to set the
reader in historical time? Who was president—king—what were
the national issues, scandals, headlines of the day, what was
being written, what was being read? Who were the popular
and avant garde artists? Did they have electric lights yet? Cars
or horses and carriages? What were wages, hours of work, size
of household staffs at various economic levels?" Her questions
and commentary provided depth to the diary's history.

Jackie writes to Louis: "As it now stands it is a book that should
be privately printed. It is a book by one of that world for that
world. It lacks interest to the general reader because the gilded
world in which the diarist lives is naturally taken for granted by
her, so there is not the appraisal and description of it which would
interest people who are not of that world."

The long and detailed editorial changes and suggestions
were virtually all adopted by Auchincloss. She advised the author to remove the clumsy footnotes, Jackie notes: "I found
these annoying, to be interrupted and look down to read. I'll
pluck one at random: Adele's cousin, daughter of her uncle
Henry T. Sloane, later Mrs. George Widener. This is irritating
because it is confusing and not information one wants to retain
unless one is a genealogist."

Although she requested to remove the footnotes, she points
out a remarkable similarity to her own upbringing revealing her
personal interest in the diary: "It reminds me of listening to Mrs.
Whitehouse and mummy talking at Bailey's Beach in Newport,
about what Charlie Whitehouse calls "tribalism." I think tribalism
is interesting and you might want to discuss it somewhere. How
important it was for everyone to know who everyone was."

Jackie notes: "Being an Edith Wharton fan from way back
there was no way I wouldn't enjoy a diary from this period, but
even beyond my own interest in this period I found myself being

involved in Florence Adele as a young woman of another period and time. She was bright, articulated and frustrated as hell at times with her own life. There are virtually no published diaries of that period available. The upper class woman was the most strictly guarded of all. Could you put in something about the rites of society—how young women were presented—how many years did they have to find a husband before they were considered old maids? Love and a happy marriage was the only adventure for these spirited protected women. She feels shut in and stifled in New York City; only in Lennox does she feel free, the wild horseback rides and picnics, her rapture with nature . . ."

After the success of *Maverick in Mauve*, Jackie hoped Louis would accept a commission to transform the Abbe Meunier diaries into another history book. Louis recalls, "It was a great many volumes of the memoirs of one of Napoleon's marshall's wives and widows. She talked to me at great length. She thought it would be a wonderful book to do!

Of course the diary had not been translated into English, and the long French verse was a challenge to decipher including enormous background research necessary to transform the diary into readable history. Louis added, "Well it was a terrific job! And those things don't pay very well. So, I told her no, and she pretended she didn't hear me! But I knew when she was listening and when she wasn't, so I repeated myself." Jackie feigned surprise, "Oh, you won't do it?" They both laughed and Louis told her, "I have no idea of doing it!"

The thing that impressed Louis was the fact that she knew about the extensive diaries, and she wasn't afraid to grasp a complex publishing idea. Louis remarked, "The mere fact that she thought somebody could undertake such a massive job interested me."

Jackie never let go of the idea that she was there to patiently guide the vision of her authors. Louis observes, "Jackie gave enormous encouragement to her writers. That's a very great thing, because an editor becomes kind of your mother. The criticism from an editor has to be quite delicately put. You expect love and encouragement from an editor, and she knew how to hand it out and at the same time she knew how make her objections stick and make you change."

THE RENAISSANCE LADY FROM AVIGNON

In June of 1993, Jackie and, her steady beau of fourteen years, Maurice Tempelsman revisited Avignon near Pont-Saint-Esprit, the ancestral village of her father Jack Bouvier's family. Avignon, once the residence of the rebel popes, Boniface VII (974) until John XXII (1316), served as a papal sanctuary near the sunny Riviera, until politically strife-torn Rome regained peace and unity. Maurice wished to revisit Arles to see the prehistoric wall-paintings in the deep caverns of Lascaux he admired in his youth. French photographers did not miss the chance to capture Jackie sailing by riverboat along the Rhone River, her picture soon appeared in Paris magazines.

The journey was abruptly cut short a few days when she became sick with the flu. She came back home to the States, and her usual routine: bright summer months in Martha's Vineyard, the golden autumn horse season in Peapack, Christmas in New York, and her treasured time with her authors. Her summer flu lingered and was later diagnosed as non-Hodgkin's lymphoma. After a year of fighting the cancer, she passed away into a peaceful sleep, as her friends read passages from Isak Dinesen, Colette and Jean Rhys. After her death, the television images of the sixty-four years after her birth on July 28th, 1929 captured a new vision of how Americans define themselves. Her foreign travel, ideas about civic planning, historic preservation of the White House, Grand Central,

Egyptian temples, and the museum as family entertainment, was a call to America to celebrate her rare excitement in a cultural adventure.

Her cultural ally, Karl Katz murmured, "They auctioned off the relics of a saint." In April of 1996, Sotheby's auctioned hundreds of histories, biographies, rare and impossible to locate oversized art books and volumes dedicated to Jackie. Illustrious authors including President Kennedy, Bernard Berenson, Andre Malraux, Churchill, Ben Gurion and virtually everyone who wrote difficult to find 20th century books were auctioned in sets categorized by topic. It seemed that all her books might serve some historical purpose if donated as a rare collection of the private library of the most famous women in the world. All the great passions and stories of her life are in those books.

"I was so intrigued by Jackie's stories, that I sat down, wrote her a letter about a year before she died. None of us knew that was in the cards at all. I wrote, 'Jackie, I had been thinking about what you know, those wonderful stories you've told and how important it is that they be remembered.'" George Plimpton's letter was mailed to Martha's Vineyard, Red Gate Farm, in the early summer of 1993.

Plimpton's letter was a plea to allow one of her oldest family friends to record the tales of her life: "Suppose this summer I come with a tape recorder and we'll just sit around—and we won't do it for anybody—we won't even tell anybody. We won't talk to a publisher. Just you reminiscing and maybe I'll do some reminiscing too. I'll talk about the night with the saxophones. I didn't say that but really just simply trying to get her to tell these stories, because, to my knowledge she has never told anybody. And there are hundreds and hundreds of them."

He wrote in his letter, "As far as I'm concerned this is a document that you can lock in a safe and I'll never even speak to anybody about it. And one day, you can will it to your grand children, if you want to, or your children. But you simply can't let these things go. I sent this letter off."

"Jackie," George, shakes his head, "wrote back this wonderful letter. She wrote that she was sitting at a desk, and she was looking out her window at this field in Martha's Vineyard—which is a wonderful place. A great meadow that flows down into the sea. And she said, that she couldn't imagine herself sitting at this desk, doing such a thing, but that she could only see herself riding through these fields on a horse."

"I was very sad to receive that letter, because it would have been a record. I was always very sorry. My own feeling is that maybe in a couple more years, she would have done it. Because I don't think you can be an editor and work with words, and do all that, that she did so well, without thinking, I've got a pretty good story here myself."

The summer of 1993, Jackie was absorbed in her life, breaking new ground with her authors and cherishing her close bonds with her family. A paradise Jackie helped inspire, the Vineyard glimmers in the crashing, high seas of American politics like a flashing beacon signaling a way back home to a lighthouse manned by liberal intellectuals who carry the sixties idealism with a stoicism like Henry David Thoreau. A long-time resident of the island, and one of Jackie's authors Dorothy West held court in the Highlands, Rose and Bill Styron and Lady Byrd Johnson anquor the northeast area of the island and Jackie's four-hundred and eighty-five acre fortress secures the island's southern jetty called Gay's Head. Jackie's friends Carly Simon, Katherine Graham, Diane Sawyer and Mike Nichols live somewhere in the middle.

Dorothy West, self-described as, "born and bred in a very special circle of colored Bostonians to whom the now descriptive word black had not yet been invented as a rallying cry . . ." was one of the aging African American writers from Jimmy Baldwin's era. Dorothy presented Jackie with an unpublished manuscript *The Wedding* and the two women "bonded in a miraculous way." Jackie loved the story and its characters, recommended the book to Doubleday, and became Dorothy's editor.

Katherine Graham, the real life heroine in the film *All the*

President's Men, shared struggles similar to Jackie's at the same moment in history. In the end, both women discovered rewarding paths: one as a newspaper publisher, and the other as a book editor. Katherine Graham was a witness to Jackie's life recalling, in her Pulitzer Prize winning autobiography *Personal History*, William (Bill) Walton's appointment as head of the Fine Arts Commission. Bill Walton became Jackie's key advisor on her efforts to restore Pennsylvania Avenue, and preserve Lafayette Square. After the White House years, Jackie commissioned his book *A Civil War Courtship: The Letters of Edwin Weller from Antietam to Atlanta*, a family diary he inherited.

The stories Katherine Graham reveal about Jackie are both humorous, and insightful. One evening, Phil Graham remarked to Jackie in the Blue Room, "Jackie, it's even better this evening to be here. I loved it the first time, but I felt sort of tense." Jackie in her smooth, frothy voice, gushed, "And now you just think it's Hamburger Heaven?"

In 1958, after the successful publication of John Kenneth Galbraith's *The Affluent Society*, Phil Graham discovered a book on Algeria by a French writer Germaine Tillon, *Algeria*. He recommended her history to all his friends including John Kennedy and Lyndon Johnson. In his note to Kennedy, he jokes: "I am sending you a little book which you can read in one hour, while Jackie should only need fifteen minutes . . ."

Both women had similar trajectories; they married brilliant men, their husbands vanished in the midst of their genius, and both wives refashioned a world raising children alone, discovering a deep satisfaction in their professions.

Joseph Alsop, a close confident of Katherine and Phil Graham and one of the first guests to dine privately with the President and First Lady, remembers his impressions: "Numerous Kennedy narratives invariably convey . . . a breathless time, full of promise and energy, and oddly enough, glamour, which is not usually associated with Washington. Try as I might, I can not contradict these accounts, nor can I look back at that period without the most unabashed feelings of romantic nostalgia and delight . . ."

President Kennedy attended Phil Graham's funeral on August 6, 1963, and Katherine Graham writes in her memoirs, "Jackie wrote me, an eight page letter, one of the most understanding and comforting of any I received . . . Just a few days after Phil's funeral Jackie gave birth to a baby boy, Patrick, who died." As one of the first women to manage a national newspaper, *The Washington Post*, and a friend of Jackie's, Graham reveals in her memoirs to be a loyal friend with a spirited courage and a determination so committed, she was undefeatable. In many ways, Jackie was this kind of person too.

Theodore Sorenson in his history *Kennedy* observes: "Jacqueline Kennedy, sensitive but strong-willed . . . by maintaining her own unique identity and provocative personality . . . by refusing to appear more folksy at political rallies or less glamourous in poorer nations, by carrying her pursuit of excellence and beauty into the White House dinners . . . she became a world-wide symbol of American culture and good taste, and offered proof in the modern age that the female sex can succeed by merely remaining feminine."

Carly Simon, with Jackie as her editor, wrote a quartet of children's books illustrated by Margot Datz. *Amy the Dancing Bear, The Boy of the Bells, The Fisherman's Song* and *The Nighttime Chauffeur* address adult themes in a child's story. *The Fisherman's Song* is a fable about healing after losing love. Jacqueline Onassis rarely edited children's books, and these are the only ones that are truly written for ages four to six.

Although she is revered for inspiring several generations of women to be model mothers, she did not focus on this area of humanity as a book editor.

In retrospect, her most universal gift to America may be her desire to be a good parent. In an interview she granted on January 4, 1961, her ideas on parenting proved to be both modern and traditional. Richard Avedon arrived from *Harper's Bazaar* to take pictures for an article on the new First Lady. In the article, "How to Bring Up a Happy Child", Jackie suggests that a young child memorize a piece of poetry for the mother's birthday present to stimulate the child's imagination and teach learning skills. Her televised interview with Dr. Spock celebrated his new ideas on child-rearing that seem timeless even today.

Carly Simon and Jackie joined efforts on another project for The Kennedy Center for Performing Arts. Carly Simon was commissioned to create a children's ballet *Voulez-Vous Danser?* In 1994, after Jackie's death, Carly Simon dedicated her last album *Letters Never Sent* to her friend and wrote a song in her memory. The lyrics in the song, *Touched By the Sun*, sound like a conversation she once had with Jackie.

If you want to be brave
Reach for the top of the sky
And the farthest point
On the horizon

Do you know who'll you'll meet there?
Great soldiers and seafarers, artists and dreamers
Who need to be close
Close to the sun

They need to be in danger of burning by fire

And I,
I want to get there
I want to be one
One who touched by the sun

The lyrics beg the question what does it take to be a hero? "I want to get there, I want to be one, One who is touched by the sun. . . ." It is a question that marks many rituals in modern life. When we elect a president, award a doctor, a police officer, a teacher and thank a good Samaritan. How can we know who to revere and who is worthy of momentary celebrity? Joseph Campbell, a professor at Sarah Lawrence College from 1934 to 1972, was fascinated by this area of study: ancient and modern heroes and mythology. Much of Campbell's work concerned the place of symbols in our daily lives, a subject of great interest to Jacqueline Onassis. Americans watching President Kennedy's funeral procession, the seven matched grays pulling the caisson and casket, the riderless horse, empty boots reversed, silver sword sheathed in the ancient tradition of mourning a fallen warrior, and then the pride of the nation, Jacqueline Kennedy, remain subconsciously in awe of her gallantry in the blinding public glare of a tragedy still palpable today.

In the interviews with Bill Moyers, Joseph Campbell observes that there are, "two types of deeds. One is the physical deed, in which the hero performs a courageous act in battle or saves a life. The other kind is the spiritual deed, in which the hero learns to experience the superhuman range of human spiritual life and then comes back with a message."

Jacqueline Bouvier wrote this when she was a young women, only twenty-two years old. "If I could be a sort of Overall Art Director of the Twentieth Century, watching everything from a chair hanging in space, it is their theories that I would apply to my period, their poems that I would have music and painting and ballets composed to. And they would make such good stepping stones if we thought we could climb any higher." When she became first lady, her affinity for artists who mentor, inspire, and champion other artists developed into her life's dream to become a kind of patron saint of the arts.

Jackie's memory lives on in the minds of authors like Peter Sis who remembered they once dreamed about creating a book on

Tibet. Sis' book *Tibet: Through the Red Box* was published in 1998. "This kind of fairytale for an adult audience could not have happened without her support. But now I can publish this style of book, she made that possible." Peter Sis illustrated and wrote the story of his father's journey to film the construction of a passage connecting Red China to Tibet in the Himalayas. The water-color paintings in both, *Tibet: Through the Red Box* and *The Three Golden Keys* capture the texture of illuminated manuscripts. The Tibetan adventure explores mysticism, Tibetan Buddhism confronted with Chinese Communism, and the complex mythology of an ancient civilization: "We learn that the lake where we are camping is a special place. The whole land of Tibet is considered to be a goddess. The mountains house mythical creatures and various Buddha forms. The lakes are oracle mirrors, they tell you how to advance in life."

Edith Hamilton once wrote, "Myths are early science, the result of human beings trying to understand what they saw around them." Both President Kennedy and Jackie challenged Americans to wonder, to communicate to the world why a nation must have a spiritual and intellectual life. Jackie's desire to advance American culture is tangible at The Kennedy Center for Performing Arts, and the hundreds of emerging new museums and arts foundations that redouble her efforts. The quote from Joseph Campbell's book *The Power of Myth* continues, "The usual hero adventure begins from whom something has been taken, or who feels there is something lacking in the normal experiences available or permitted to the members of society. This person then takes off on a series of adventures beyond the ordinary, either to recover what has been lost or to discover some life-giving elixir. It's usually a cycle, a going and a returning . . . That's the basic motif of the universal hero's journey, leaving one condition and finding the source of life to bring you forth into a richer or more mature condition."

"She's very special for me," Peter Sis savors the last time he saw his editor Mrs. Onassis, "If anyone wants to know what is the fulfillment of my life in New York, it was when I brought in the pictures for our book. We put them all over the conference room at Doubleday. While she looked at the pictures, I could see Times Square behind her. I felt this is wonderful. This is the American dream come true."

Jackie said, "Thank you, thank you," and she had tears in her eyes.

Peter offered, "I have to dedicate this book to you."

She said, "No, it's your book, and it's a beautiful book and it's for your daughter, Madeleine."

"So in May, when she so unexpectedly for me at least, was gone, I put in just a little line, thank you for a dream J.O."

The Prophecy of Isaiah, 701 B.C.
Old Testament

And they shall
beat their swords into
ploughshares
And their spears into
pruninghooks
Nation shall not lift up
sword against
nation
Neither shall they
learn war
evermore.

And they shall see 'eye to eye' . . .

This book is dedicated to Jacqueline Bouvier Kennedy
and President John F. Kennedy for their shared belief
in the vision of Isaiah.

Jackie: Beyond the Myth of Camelot is based exclusively on K.L. Kelleher's copyrighted materials, personal research, study, observations, conversations, and correspondence.

The national press heralded the PBS broadcast of
Jackie: Behind the Myth on November 29th, 1999, a landmark
documentary inspired by Karl Katz, Suzanne Bauman
and Karen Kelleher's determination to reveal the true record
of a woman's rare vision and champion of diverse culture.

Jackie: Behind the Myth

"Show of the Week."
                People

" . . . a brilliant woman who overcame almost unthinkable tragedies to become a highly effective champion of culture, historic preservation and quality books."
                New York Daily News

"Throughout her youth, she was encouraged by her grandfather, who managed to get her poetry published in the East Hampton Star when she was eight . . ."
                East Hampton Star

"It's simply about art and beauty and an inspiring woman who loved both."
                The Record, New Jersey

"I was through mourning Kennedys but this lyrical biography stirs familiar feelings of loss."
                TV Guide

"She fascinated such prominent leaders as DeGaulle, Khrushchev and Nehru and became a genuine goodwill ambassador to nations around the world."
                WTTW Eleven, Chicago

Printed in the United States
2524